Presidential Treason of Three Stooges

President Clinton
President Bush and
President Obama
for
Aiding Islamic Terrorists

New Updated March 2017

By Lawrence A. Lueder 2017

Also by (Lawrence A. Lueder)

A 1950s American Childhood in Morocco
NAVSSES
NAVSEA
Sunaru Infinite Planet
The Criminal Part 1-6

None of this book may be copied without explicit written authorization from the author or his representatives.

Copyright © 2017 by Lawrence A. Lueder
All rights Reserved.
ISBN-13: 978-1544008615
ISBN-10: 1544008619
Library of Congress Number: **2017900959**

Introduction

Salami Rushdie, Gen. **James Mattis, Bridgette Gabriel, David Wood**, and so many others, I thank you all including the various websites where I downloaded lists of Islamic terrorism. The lists are too large to list them all and still make this book affordable. Also many thanks to all of you that posted videos burning the Quran, I have yet to burn my copy of the Quran and post it too. Please visit their sites of truth about the evils of Islam on YouTube or visit the internet to learn much more. Many thanks to Heidi Munn, of Germany for saving her church from the evil Muslim intruders. Islamic terrorism is exploding exponentially, and if not stopped will be the foundation for the next major World War. Below I go into some brief history about the Butcher Muhammad, prove that he is not a prophet, show that the Quran is all garbage and explain why Europe and North America needs to put an end to all Muslim activities including the dismantling of all mosques throughout the United States. Places like England and some of the Germanic countries are slowly waking up to the dangers Islam poses to this country. Rape, murder, theft and property destruction is at an all-time high because of Muslims immigrants. These are not terrorist Muslims; these are just plain old Muslims pretending to be peaceful and are Europe's dilemmas. The mistake England made was to assume that if they diversified like America that it would also gain from the diversity. However, the opposite is happening. Being a much smaller area than the U.S., England and other European countries is a test tube of things to come in America. This book is a wakeup call to Washington to stop whitewashing Muslim bad behaviors and to reverse avoidance of publishing negative news and speech against misinformed Muslims. No other religion in the world is as dangerous as Islam, costing every nation of the world hundreds of billions of dollars fighting it each year. Congress must take the lead away from political correctness; otherwise, all free US citizens should arm themselves for the war against Islam to come. I also blame many of our presidents for aiding Muslim terrorist around the world.

Before we can go on to investigate the presidents for treason, we must first look at the history of Muhammad and learn something about the Quran.

What is known about Muhammad?

This is my book, and I'll translate it in ways most intelligent people see religion, and not by some that hold on to some mystical Universal God, which never seems to show himself in any form or miracle. Shame on those people that protect and aided in rebuilding Mosques that were burned in America for you fools have not read the Quran. When your sons are murdered, fighting evil Muslims remember you were warned. When you praise Muslims that cut off the heads of innocent Christians, make sure that you let their mothers know that you approve of such barbaric Islamic behavior by helping them rebuild. To praise Muslims entering America is to approve of more violence such as the murder of innocent people by nut job Muslims that get offended from witnessing freedom in America, and you condone pedophilia, shameful illiterate Americans.

First off, back in the past when all the humans were, basically, illiterate about the world, it was easy to conjure up a God, and Gods came in all forms from nature to the sky to animals and even stones. You get the picture.

As man started farming and constructing communities there evolved a need for order, hence leaders such as kings were made, men who would have the ultimate say on how things should be, in order for everyone to get along. For those areas that were conquered or even remote for social order, something else was needed. Far away from communities and such, there was no law, so one was made which involved a God of unimaginable powers. Often it was a God, that could determine how you would spend the rest of eternity after death, in some form of either hell, or in paradise, and there was other punishment or benefits to behaving according to society's culture and rules.

You can spew all the ancient literatures you want, most of them if not all were written on some leafy parchment, goatskins or even stone, that's how perfect it is to many, simply rubbish. Muslims are the dumbest of all claiming their Quran is the last gospel and the best ever written, and it was never changed, it is so perfect. Really? Spend a few moments on YouTube and you will be educated that in fact there are many copies of the Quran all different. Get over it and stop lying to the people, you asshole mullahs.

Yes, many of the religious texts have some good written history, and some have good rules to live by, which many of us understand without any religious reading of such literature, or baptism or the drinking of special wine. But that's about it, unless, you are foolish enough to believe it and want to subject yourself to a life with limits, a caged bird perhaps or a chained dog trained to attack should anyone doubt the word of God/Allah, which Muslims often do. To say, God Damn, as many of us have often said, we were told that to say such negativity that God would send us to hell.

Let's see how great your God is. Where was God when millions of Jews were being murdered by the Nazi? Before I forget some of my hard to get along with religious friends, and I got into a discussion about religion. Right off the bat, they start spewing religious facts as if they know it all. When I was able to get a word in edge wise I simply said, "Where was God during the Vietnam War or in the killing fields of Cambodia? Where was God when the nuclear bombs were dropped on Japan, or when Pearl Harbor was being attacked as Americans celebrated the birth of Jesus Christ, God's son? If God/Allah loves his creations so much, why are they all butchering each other in the Middle East, each side claiming their God is the better one. One friend would not let me finish as he blabbered on and on asking silly things, like how many books make up the Old Testament. I didn't know and I didn't care, that's not what I was trying say. He refused to allow me to talk over the phone after I repeatedly asked him, so I simply did what most of us do and hung up. Good health is all you need. Back to ...

Wouldn't you know it just after completing the first draft I, suddenly, had a heart attack? Aren't these hospitals great, I was in and out in five days. Anyway, this book is some of the fixes and additions. Continue...

So where is God that he only revealed himself or spoke to humans when they were uneducated, illiterate, much like the people of Central Africa is today or the Jungle Indians from South America etc. What is keeping God from speaking with us today? Some might say that he does, he does it in unexplainable miracles like when someone is about to die, then suddenly, awakens all cured or whatever. Maybe we still aren't quite there yet in our intelligent to understand such causes of miracles as some people see them. Just like floods, earthquakes, and other disasters were considered punishments by God. Jews like to claim that the reason so many died under the Nazis was that God was punishing them for not sticking to the guidelines, as set forth by their religious teachings.

Also, Jews believe or often claim that they are the most intelligent beings. Personally, maybe I'm a bit racist, I believe Germans were much more intelligent and I see a lot of great stuff being developed by the Japanese, but you don't see hardly anything coming out of Israel. At least not anything, that seems to benefit the world. Prestigious Awards in science they may have many, however, once you know what is required to get one the rest is easy. Most great inventors cannot be bothered with knowing how to write scientific articles, whereas the Jews must know the format. Once I wrote my first patent the rest were easy. Yes, I have several patents, and I did not need a lawyer to write it as the majority of people do. And to dress in Quaker like hats while sporting ridiculous braids shows truly how ridiculous Hasidic Jews are, not to mention treating their women as second class citizens.

If Jews were, so intelligent they would purchase land anywhere else in the world and move there away from lands that saw more bloodshed than any other place in the world. There is nothing holy about Jerusalem; it is a place of death. By the way, if God loved the Jews so much, why does Jewish land have nothing while all the Arabs/Muslims have all the oil? Jews have so little to survive, that they rely heavily on the US for billions of dollars every years. You know what is considered Holy land, North America. That's right, America has everything and more peace than most places in the world considering the diversity of people and cultures. Personally, the Jews could buy land in such places as South America, Australia etc. and move away from death every day, and move far away from idiots that believe in the Butcher Muhammad, the phony prophet as proven in their own Quran. By the way, none of the Jewish prophets was without sin, all of them had committed murder, which makes you wonder as to why Jews and the Muslims keep at each other's throats and both consider the same dirt sacred.

Another problem with some of the Jews that I see on television and other media is that they fail in exposing Islam as a cult. Why is it that most of the videos posted that depict the negatives about Islam seem to be from non-Muslim British and American citizens? I thought the Jews were supposed to be the experts in examining in detail ancient artifacts and literature. And why is it even in America that I see Jews often lending a hand to rebuild a mosque that might have been burned or whatever. I'm not proposing a Nazi stance, only that there should be a mutual assist. However, what you see always is a one sided help coming from the Jewish communities.

Another possibility is for Israel to become one of our states, the 51 state. Just think of the benefits and get away from believing the area is so special. Same thing for Mexico, using our system of governing there wouldn't be as many problems as they presently have from corruption, and the list of ills can go on... Yuck, I know some of you...

I might also suggest that the Israeli stop trying to bomb the Palestinians to make changes for the better and try something different. Try advertising in bold signs, near the wall, verses from the Quran in three different languages. Start with the verse that says; kill the infidels or the one that says women are stupid or should be whipped and beaten. I believe the more this kind of information is out there, the more Muslims will see they need to change. I like a sign that says Jesus never murdered anyone; however, Muhammad did murder thousands, robbed and had many slaves. It's guaranteed to work. Bombs only make them run to fight another day. You have to go after the brainwashed Muslims with the truth. The majority of Muslims live in the darkness of intelligence, hence their pent-up anger. Oh, and here is another good saying; why do you cover up your women? Is it because they are too ugly for the rest of the world to see?

Back to: while we are at it, let's say something about Moses. Aah yes here is a man that was supposed to be so holy that if you look at his history, you will note that this douche bag murdered thousands of innocent people himself. I do not recall the religious historian that was on TV speaking about Moses, but I believe his version was more realistic and true, than all others stories that portrayed Moses as a man who spoke with God and saved his people. Really? First off, a talking bush, that's like the talking snaking in Adam and Eve. And why would a God write down his words on stone tablets, what happened to an IPad or even written in gold like the other douche bags, the Mormons prophet, just to prove he was God. After receiving, the Ten Commandments Moses had all the idol worshippers slaughtered. From there he went from village to village slaughtering everyone including the women and children while always claiming the lands were given to his people by God. Don't forget, Moses was a trained warrior from Egypt, he knew how to fight and kill. Moses was more like Muhammad, a butcher and a thief. After a dozen or so villages ravaged, it seems no one knows what happened to Moses. Some believe, and it makes more sense that his own military people murdered him, because they were not going to kill any more babies as Moses had commanded. Somehow, it had psychologically bothered them, and that they had to do something to stop the murder of innocent babies. So there you go, nothing holy about Moses. In addition, if Moses was true, the only reason the Pharos chased after Moses was because, when Moses left with his people, all of them stole what they could carry before departing. They took valuable tools, weapons, food and anything of value. I might include that there is no proof that Moses ever existed, but historians keep looking. Sure, they find artifacts at the bottom of the Red Sea and such items but still nothing. Moses was more of a good story that was told to provide hope for the commoner, but also the story provided a way in which the people should live their life's and more. Rulers were brutal individuals in those days and a story about a lone man getting away as Moses did was something to dream about. Let's not forget that Moses walked around for 40 years looking for the promised land, what happen to God simply showing Moses where to go by including a map with the commandments? In 40 years, you can walk across America a good 50 times. And we now know what caused all those plagues that struck during the dark ages, which can easily account for those that Moses was blamed for making. People were dirty, non-hygienic and superstitious back then. It's easy to blame the invisible man in the sky when things go wrong and take it out on the innocent as the cause of God's wrath. As a child first seeing Charlton Hesston play Moses in the Movies, I believed everything in it too.

The other Bible story is Noah's Ark and the great flood. Really? You would need a ship the size of a football field, maybe bigger, to fit two of each kind of animal, not to mention all the feed for 30 days. If God told Noah to build the boat, why couldn't God just make it rain where there were bad people? Why was the whole earth flooded? After all, he's God he can do anything. God could have easily provided a motorized boat already filled with animals and enough fuel to reach America. Now that's a God to me. Sounds more as if aliens witnessed what was about to occur in the Mediterranean Sea and warned Norah to get ready if anything. Scientist now knows that the Med. drained roughly three or four times in the past, because the strait of Gibraltar closed and opened. The opening and closing would have caused floods including other such natural disasters, such as huge earthquakes. If there was some kind of huge boat, it no doubt only held domestic animals. Which at that time were all the animals Noah would have known about? I am sure Noah never saw a North American Bison or a lemur from Madagascar. All stories, as was the Trojan horse...keep on looking dreamers.

Let's get off saving people for a tad. Where is God to protect all the wildlife that is disappearing in places like Africa, and what about the cruelty of animals in slaughterhouses? Who speaks for them? Some of the most cruelty to animals is perpetrated by Muslims; you only need to visit their homelands to witness animals being tortured as if they have no feelings. Thank you, ignorant people in America for protecting Muslims. You evil people see nothing wrong with harming animals, after-all animals are only there to serve man and cannot possible know any difference, the way

Muslims see them. Someday take a visit to a Muslim butcher slaughterhouse before you speak. In Saudi Arabia, they have contest every years for who can kill the most birds, many of them extremely rare. Whole freezers are shown topped with beautiful song birds. Muslims aren't even allowed to have indoor pets.

Before leaving this chapter, I should remind the losers to read the story in the Quran about the 600 decapitations. Muhammad had taken sanctuary with a village that protected him. After Muhammad's enemies left the area, Muhammad had all the men of the village put to the sword. It took them three days to cut off all 600 heads. This is how shameful Muslims are to believe in such an evil man as Muhammad. When did Jesus ever murder a single person, or steal, or kept slaves?

Find Muhammad in the pile of skulls.
You won't, because he's masturbating on the pile from behind.

My apology for juxtaposing some of my text, it's just the way my brain works.
Also, without some costly editor, you get the picture.

Questions about Muhammad

Why did it take Muhammad, are you reading this Stupid Saudi Mullahs, why did it take him 22 years to get all the words from the Angel Gabriel in a cave mind you? What was the matter with the Angel Gabriel that he could not teach Muhammad how to read or write? Why didn't Gabriel just hand Muhammad a copy of what Muhammad needed to preach, after-all he is an angel, and what is the angel doing in a dirty cave of all places. What happened to Muhammad's beautiful palace or tent in those days for a place to meet Gabriel? Don't any of you Muslims even consider these thoughts? And the Biggy question, here it comes; who created God/Allah to create the world and us? In addition, if you look on the internet on YouTube there are now thousands of videos of alien spacecraft flying over earth, landing and even aliens stepping out. There is even proof that they are on the moon and on Mars, so did God create them too in his own image?

Everybody in the world from Eskimos to Africans to Greeks, they all worshipped some kind of God or many Gods in the past. Much of that had to do with the fact that we all want to live forever. We all hope that our spirit will somehow live for eternity in paradise. No one wants to feel that all their life's hard work is, suddenly, gone to become dirt. Our body fought to stay alive at all cost only to end into dust. So, spirituality of an invisible place is better than no place at all. Spirituality also provides a sense of order for the mind that is ever questioning; it's that mysterious father that tells us to behave or else.

Spirituality does not always work as is seen with the Cristian Crusaders, the Inquisition, Jihad attacks by Muslims, and so forth.

Forget about the adult people that died horribly from waring issues, what about the children who were murdered, by people fighting over which has the best God? Defenders of their ideology often behave like children; my Daddy can beat up your Daddy. Where is God protecting the innocent children? How many have to perish before once again so called Gods shows themselves?

If Muslims believe God/Allah created man, why are Muslims placing a bag over the woman for no one to see her except for her husband? She is God's creation not man's creation, just as God created the flower and the beautiful creatures from birds to the handsome horses none of those are covered. To cover up a woman is shameful behavior, there is nothing to be ashamed of and it is only man covering up the woman as if she is his personal toy or property. Her body is so special there is no other like hers and only I the moronic idiot of a husband can look at it. You never see Muslims women enjoying themselves like all other women that are not Muslim, laughing, singing, dancing and anything they want to do. God created man and woman as equals if you believe in God, so stop being a jerk asshole repressive Muslims. No wonder you Muslims are always at each other's throat, you're never enjoying life. With all the porno shit on the internet, what makes you Muslims think that your woman's body is any different that requires a cover-up? I can understand the bag, if your woman looks like some goat, but then again some people like that goat look.

It has been refreshing to see some of the Muslim scholars, on YouTube, that are finally speaking out against the constant forced teaching of that awful evil book the Quran. They are claiming the Quran is what is causing young boys to commit the murders of innocent people, and it causes their countries to be non-productive in everything.

In Afghanistan, our military should have been handing out sample magazines of any kind from the free world, so that the repressed could see the truth. A Bible would have been nice but since we had mud heads for presidents, our government bends over for Muslims to stick it to them. Can you imagine? Here we are the greatest power in the world and some scums with rotten teeth and wearing flip-flops can bring America to kneel like some trained animal. Shame on all my presidents, from Eisenhower up until Obama, the worst of all, for being such pussies. Just before leaving office, Obama approved the sale of some 15 billion in arms to Saudi Arabia. The Saudi were known to use these same weapons to indiscriminately bomb innocent civilians, such as those people in Yemen. Saudi also funded Sunni terrorist, still practice slavery and all that is socially ugly. It's as if our presidents didn't give a shit for women being beating in public to having acid thrown on her face and many other such ills.

This is a good time to mention Evil Hillary Clinton; are you people that voted for her stupid or what? How many of you knew that she was receiving money from the evil Muslims regimes such as the Saudi and from Morocco. Why would you want to see more bombings in the Middle East and all that death, all of it occurred because of people like Obama supplying arms to terrorist like the Saudi and Pakistan, both countries that do nothing to stop forcing people to memorize the stinking Quran, the very book responsible for 100% of the Muslim killings World Wide. Hillary voters owe the FREE Americans an apology for being ignorant of the Qurans' teachings. I find it shameful of the people that voted for Hillary. It was also shameful of the crooked News media for not publishing the truth about how evil Hillary was in accepting money from terrorist. If elected, she would have guaranteed arms for the terrorist Islamic religion over all other religions.

People reading this please understand that our presidents although well intentioned in the beginning of their term, all made historical mistakes which eventually caused many of our soldiers to die protecting evil dictators, Mullahs and such twisted places of worship like Mecca. America should have known better ever since we broke away from Britain. The breakaway wasn't because of taxes as history will have us believe, it was more to do with learning to live on your own, as most children do after they pass their teenage years. Islam on the other hand, does not allow anyone to leave and will meter out death to those that do and death to those that do not believe in their ways. Forcing prayer five times, a day is pure brainwashing. No free world countries should deal with those that use such repressive religions as Islam.

America blindly allowed the repression of millions of people to continue much like it ignored Hitler's rise to power. Now that Islam has spread worldwide, America fumbles to react using political correctness, a feather you might say. It was the few that remained silent in Germany that allowed a psychopath like Hitler to exist.

I like what some commanders are suggesting, hit them hard and fast and do it so that they will never forget into eternity, when the world is no more. Going after that single person each time is like going after one of the scorpions' babies, you never know when one day; one of those scorpions will get you hidden in one of your shoes. A bus full of passengers, or school kids, an event where many are having a good time are potential targets, why wait Mr. President? Begin taking away some of the Qurans and closing down Islamic schools. These types of attacks have been happening in Israel and you believe we are safe Mr. President? Did America forget 9/11 already? It only took a handful of Muslims to murder thousands in ONE DAY.

The media is also fully responsible for what happened on 9/11. Yes they are, like CNN, The NY Times, etc. All of you cowards have no problem attacking the Catholic Church for child molesting but you have yet to say negatives about the Quran, the heart of the Islamic teachings as the sole source of Islamic evil deeds.

Throughout the US the Saudi have built compounds surrounded by armed guards for guerilla warfare training for the Muslims, all disguised as Mosques. Why the guns Mr. President, you say they are peaceful? So were Jones Town and the Branch Davidian organizations/religions.

In the wake of all the refugees migrating to Europe and other parts of the world, why are they not migrating to Saudi Arabia, next door? Why is no one asking that question? Is it because they fear the Saudi way of life? On the other hand, are the Saudi faking it again thereby making the free world feed and house all those lost Muslims soles. It's the Saudi way of getting the maximum number of Muslims into free land areas, where they can gradually force their Islamic ways on our societies. Make no mistake the Saudi are calculating into the future for their repressive way of existence.

It you doubt the Saudi are not part of ISIS, ask yourself this: when was the last time anyone heard of a Saudi out on the front lines battling the terrorist? However, it's okay for our ex-presidents to send in our boys to do the Saudi's dirty work. The Saudi were playing with fire and now the fire has gotten out of hand, witness the Middle East in fighting everywhere.

By the way, in case you are wondering, no, I am not an atheist; I was born with a mother that was Catholic. She spent time with nuns in Sicily during WWII. Dad was more of an atheist, but kept to himself, a quiet man. I learned the various Catholic prayers on my own and I can recite many of them. Mother was not much of a churchgoer except for Easter and Christmas, and she never taught any of her children much about Christianity. Therefore, you could say I was a Christian believer on my own because Christianity was so positive and it made a lot of sense in how we should live life. I even memorized many of the prayers. When I got married, I attended church with my wife for many years and then stopped going because I felt God is in the heart. A sip of wine and the taste of a cracker do not make one religious, it just fills an inner sole need to belong, I suppose. My wife has never stopped going to church. As I got older, I began to see life differently with more questions. Priest molesting young boys, Bunga-Bunga parties the Cardinals in Rome were attending and so on. Many of the Protestant ministers I consider crooks that live lavish lives. I found it more enlightening to believe in yourself, as long as you do good deeds what do you have to fear if there is a heaven. You do not need a priest to tell you what is right or wrong, especially from one without a clean sole himself. What about people preachers like Indira Gandhi from India, I doubt that God would not accept him because he was not a Christian or had communion. Think...

What I believe is a more plausible God.

What I believe makes more sense is that we were placed here or genetically altered here by aliens from another place in the universe, and I tell you why. Why, because even though they try to teach us evolution in school some of it makes sense. We can alter a dog to look differently in many ways as we do livestock and other animals. What does not make sense is what happened to all those in-between apes that we supposedly came from. Humans could not have possible murdered them all; there would have been more walking upright apes verses people even today. For example, there are many different species of deer, horses, birds, and so on. Even in places like central Africa, in the past there were millions of wildebeests, elephants and many other animals, until humans began to replace them. Even today, you would be hard pressed to find hairy people outside of some Persians or Greeks. By the way, the Greeks were gene hijacked during the Greek and Persian wars. Hairy people would have been as numerous as Black people that are mixed in with the Caucasian world populations as in the present.

No, it seems more likely that we were placed on earth and left to find our own way. It would explain why we developed so quickly from mud huts to skyscrapers in a few thousand/hundred years. It explains how we discovered DNA sequences in such a short time frame, or how we landed on the Moon and Mars, and so many other discoveries like computers. It also explains why the Pyramids and other such structures around the world all look similar and has similar uses. It is too coincidental that humans halfway around the world had similar thoughts, such as we all came from the stars.

Some might ask, why don't the aliens show themselves or come in contact to help us have a better life. Well, it's not so easy. Put it this way, if you were to place humans on another planet, do you really think those people would want you meddling into their affairs? Remember when America was settled, we wanted no interference from Britain... Once you help them, they would cease to learn to better themselves and would continue to worship the aliens' verses working to get what they need. A dog does that, they beg and we humans feed them and medicate them as needed. Sure there are working dogs, I'm writing about dogs in general, which also explains why people from struggling countries notice the dogs behavior or mannerisms better than people that seem to have it all or the good life.

By not interfering with humans aliens can stand back and take advantage of stuff humans have discovered. The more people planets, the more knowledge they gain. We here on earth learn from one another, I venture to guess that the free world like America and Europe provides much of the knowledge gains. Now, imagine creatures that use thousands of inhabited planets for their knowledge.

Just as a dog or most animals has a built in set of survival instincts, such as giving birth to puppies and knowing without any outside influences, how to nurture and take care of its litter. We humans have a similar instinct that there is something bigger out there in space, and we do what we can to reach the stars from building pyramids to rocket ships.

Checkout YouTube, there are now thousands of videos showing flying saucers and other weird craft not of this earth. Many of these videos are updated daily from around the world. Some no doubt fake; however, others seem impossible to fake.

I might also mention that I saw an alien when I was about five years old and we were living in Morocco at the time. I wrote about it in my first book, *A 1950s American Childhood in Morocco*. In addition, one day when we were living in North Dakota my brother Lou and I, were on the back steps looking up at the night sky, when, suddenly, we saw three saucers fly by in close formation, and at very high speed. Enough of that...

Living 12 years in Morocco I grew up with Muslim kids. I went hunting for birds with them (not killing – trapping) and slept overnight with them and more. Yes, they were great friends, but no one was forced into any religion that I can recall. It was just a hand full that we ever saw attending a Mosque here and there. Many of the women were not fully covered and many of them actually embraced dressing European. Believe me when I say, it was the Saudi with their evil sticky fingers paying off the Moroccan government to build more Mosques, and they were paying to teach the shit-hole Sharia laws in the areas. And it all goes back to the British and Americans that put them into power. Not once did any American or European country ever try to get the Muslim countries to ease up or change for the better. What you are seeing happening in the Arab world is over the years, Muslims have been able to build up arms to where they now feel they can intimidate any of the super powers. Make no mistake; America has not seen the worst of the Muslims world and its destructive capabilities.

Military historians fail to recall how America ignored what was happening in Europe when Hitler came to power, and it was all because of a single mind thought, NAZI are the superior race. This is exactly what the Muslims say and enforce on others wherever they can. Islam is the only true religion and the Quran is superior to all other religious text. Sounds like Hitler to me – I suppose Washington requires another major Islamic attack to WAKE THE FUCK UP! See Bridgette Gabriel on YouTube for a better explanation.

In their own Muslim country, they have managed to expel all those from other religions through intimidations or various other negatives. In much of Europe, they enforce their own sharia laws, they take over whole neighborhoods, and they attack any outsider. Women are being raped in Europe in unpresented numbers never seen before; I believe the majority is committed by Muslims. Is this what Washington wants to see occur in the US?

In France 2017, they are having elections and Marine Le Pen is running for president on a platform to stop any further Muslim invasion. Paris and it beautiful Mediterranean beaches is not France when Muslims try to impose their ways, with burkinis on the beaches. Also, she hopes to stop Muslims and Indians from wearing turbans. Religious customs only brings with it a fight. And so far she is winning as I am writing these changes. Some call her the Donald Trump of France.

The Muslims are the majority on their own turf, but in the free world, they make up a small percentage with a very **loud voice** and enforcement of **Sharia**.

History of Muhammad

The truth about how Islam got its start does not exactly begin, or I should say, stayed in power from the early 600 up until today. Actually, Islam had at one time practically vanished during the beginning of the1900. What propped it up again was the free world. Yes, that's right, it was the stupid British government to be exact with the help of the Americans during World War II. Remember, Lawrence of Arabia, history labeled him a hero who fought with the Arabs against the Turkish invasion in the lands we now know as Saudi Arabia. The Brits foolishly agreed to help a bunch of illiterate crooks, men that rode camels and robbed from anyone they could. It was and still is the way much of the Arab world works even today. Once in power, what better way to control the people, than to force them to memorize the Quran, as Hitler had done with is vision of world dominance? A book that tells them to keep on murdering, robbing and slavery is how followers of Islam held on to power. Speaking of slavery ex-presidents, how is it that you can celebrated Black History month, while at the same time supply arms to bunch of degenerates like the Pakistani or the Saudi, least I don't forget the Malaysians or the Turks. That's like saying, thanks for getting us all those Negro slaves back in history.

Guess what, the internet is slowly but surely allowing the repressed to read the truth. No thanks, to the British who also were responsible for forcing Chinese to use drugs; you Brits are not as innocent and proper as you profess. You did not look at the big picture, as the US did not see it as well, in all its encounters in the Middle East Wars. What America did thanks to Stupid and idiot Presidents like the Bushes, Clinton, and Obama was to take out the gang leaders and then left the countries to the gang members to fight for power, very stupid indeed my presidents and their stupid, idiot advisors.

Arabs were also considered responsible for destroying all the agriculture that dominated the Mediterranean coast during Muhammad's time. The reason why was because, Arabs were camel jockeys often raiding one another for booty. None of them knew how to farm and saw that they could make more money by stealing it from others. Gangs work in similar fashion. Much of the Muslims to this day are still involved in sophisticated crimes, kidnapping for ransom, drugs and anything illegal that they can get away with in the free countries, like the US and Europe. Where there is oil in the Muslim countries, much of the revenue is doled out to those that support the repressive regime, which explains why they fervently fight to keep the same ass-hole leader in power, at all cost, including committing murder. Sanctioned by the US and Europe with huge arms deals. I venture to guess many of our presidents received money from these same repressive dictators, to win their own election thereby ensuring the evil Muslim tyrants remained in power. You could look at it as extortion by the Americans, in that we offered protection for some of their oil money. The truth is in follow the money stupid.

Arabs not only destroyed North Africa's agriculture, they systematically are destroying every country they infect. Detroit city is a prime example of Muslims taking on many wives in secret, and then placing them all on the welfare system, each gets their own rental home too. Once their numbers increases, they take over city council, and dictate for Muslims changes. They begin to enforcing the shit Sharia laws. If Muslims were so honest and follow the rules for the countries they reside in, besides some sharia Muslim law, why haven't even one of them, ever bothered to alert the law enforcers about potential Muslim attacks or even assisted in finding perpetrators of attacks.

By the way, Britain is starting to feel the wrath of Muslims, as is France as the Islamic population goes up, which was predicted. Too bad, they did not see it coming. Washington was never prepared for the Peoples Temple run by Jim Jones 1977 that left nine Hundred people dead. What about the Branch Davidian cult, or the Heaven's Gate cult, when they made the headlines in March of 1997 when 39 members of the cult killed themselves, and what about the 77 people from Branch Davidians that were burned alive in the fire March 1993, and other similar cults. Shit for brains our the American intelligence services.

The free world not only propped up the Saudi, but also supplied them with all the tools and technology to extract oil. We did this for all the oil rich Muslim countries like Libya, Iran, Iraq, etc. So long as we (America) were getting oil, who cares what the Arabs did to suppress the people into memorizing the evil Quran. It was the Saudi way of remaining in power. What the free world should have said back then in history was; we will work with you, but you have to allow other religions to exist equally. Of all the religions in world, only Islam is repressive and evil, spewing nothing but torture and death as a way of life. Believe in the Quran, otherwise, a Muslim will be honored to murder you. How could the British, the French or even the Americans not see a problem with sanctioning one religion, and a repressive one at that? How could a country like America with such a wonderful Constitution allow another country, which it saved to be so repressive towards its people. Suddenly, the Arab people had only one choice to read and believe in, repressive Islam.

As the years went on the Arab World grew stronger, and spread farther with the tools and weapons constantly supplied by the free world, Europe, and America predominately. Thanks to Americas idiot presidents since Roosevelt. Yes, every president since WWII, either, supplied the evil Muslim tyrants' arms, and no doubt received kickbacks from sales of the arms from dealers and nobody at the time cared. We were making lots of money. Everyone in the free world was working making weapons from jets to tanks and billions of ammunitions. Muslims can't even make a simple bullet. Everything they use; is or was purchased from non-believers of the

Quran. That's because the idiot Muslims have to pray five times a day or so. When do you suppose they have time to produce anything? This has been proven so on YouTube by Muslim leaders themselves. What you will find the majority of Muslims doing is some form of corruption, stealing from one another, extortion, cheating and lying. All those negative behaviors are mentioned in the Quran as okay to do. It also tells Muslims to breed constantly in order to take over the world. Can you imagine a world with nothing but thieves and crooks? Which explains why many of the Muslins living in places like Detroit are on welfare with 10 or more children? One Muslims will secretly marry five wives and get each one pregnant, and all of them on welfare each receive housing assistance. If I repeat anything, so what.

During the Middle East Wars in Afghanistan, Iran and Syria, President at the time Obama supplied billions of dollars in arms to the stinking royal Saudi Family only to have it transferred to the ISIS terrorist through a proxy gimmick. Here's how it went, the Saudi gave the arms it received to some phony rebels, or the phony Iranian army only to have the army flee without a single shot being fired, so the terrorist could come in and take over the weapons. It was all a ruse to make it appear that Obama had nothing to do with arming ISIS terrorist. You do not arm gangs of any kind, especially Muslims bent on murdering Americans. All the stinking Saudi people are Sunni, the same kind of shit people the ISIS people were and are, Sunni. Dahh, are you reading this you idiot Obama, the terrorist supplier of arms. What happened to the Presidents oath to protect Americans?

Is anyone in Washington noticing that while some members (like Hillary Clinton) are trying to take guns away from American Citizens, they do just the opposite with repressive regimes or leaders of the Evil Muslim countries by approving huge arms sales. It is as if Hillary was telling the Muslims, "You go ahead and kill more of our military troops with these brand new weapons, while I work on this side to disarm the Americans. The two of us working together, I think we can get Americas to accept Islam." That is what she and others in Washington sounds like to me.

Stop being stupid America, we do not need to rent any Muslim airports to fight terrorist. It is time to develop flying aircraft carriers instead of lumbering costly water born behemoths that cost billions just to keep them moving each year. That's billions we can spend on infrastructures and things that are more positive. See my suggestions at my website if you dare www.larryandjane.com checkout patents.

To supply any Muslims run country with arms is like arming killer gangsters in any city of the world. It's wrong. You do not arm ass-holes like the Saudi or the Pakistani, both governments of which have been murdering people by the thousands to remain in power. How dare our presidents give any assistant to such evil people as the Muslims in Saudi Arabia or Pakistan, two Muslim countries that are known to have murdered young schoolgirls for not obeying stinking Muslim law. Saudi Arabia had schools with girls burned down and left the girls locked in because they were not wearing any head covering. The Saudi and Pakistani governing officials should be brought before the world court, and then hanged for their evil deeds of murder and forced teaching of the Quran to young innocent hungry children, all in the name of a phony God/Allah. Neither the evil Pakistani or the Saudi tried to find Osama Bin Laden or any of the other terrorist, the free world was searching for, and yet, countries like Pakistan is like the size of one of our states? Don't tell me these two ass-hole Muslim people did not know where the tall fucking killer was hiding. All the while the United States was continuing to give the extortionist Pakistani government millions of dollars each year to find him. In addition, you do not arm one religion over all others, that act is racist and against our First Amendment. Obama is a racist Negro president. By the way, I still feel his wife is a man per YouTube videos and his children are both adopted, proving once again that the stinking news media lied to the public about Michelle.

Saudi Arabia has been publishing books in the US, by US publishers, books that read hatred towards American and advocate the murder on innocent people as spelled out in the Quran. I ask Congress to please stop all such literature and make those accountable immediately.

I am not all Talk, I Have an Answer

Radio Free Europe is what eventually took down Communist Russia and no doubt got China to make changes for the better. I suggest the same for all Islamic countries, only this time we use television-broadcasting everyday with free American television shows. It's a small price to pay for peace in the world. It should also be applied against North Korea. Any channel that gets blocked, America should reciprocate and block some of their broadcast, in retaliation. Presently, Saudi Arabia and Pakistan avoid showing their people the truth much as the communist Russians did in the past. America should lead in this area, the radios that were issued in Afghanistan was a mere drop in the bucket for change. Not everyone can afford the internet in such areas but Television is another matter. Whether they use analog or digital television, we should transmit Freedom Television. I am sure that such an endeavor would have no difficulty-acquiring sponsors. It sure beats flying drones for hundreds of millions of Dollars using taxpayer money or sending in our boys to fix the mess. It's better than what they have been doing or using.

There should be programs on television that show the Afghan people why drugs are bad, and show them another way to start other form of businesses. Show them space, and science is how you awaken and change minds that are presently being brainwashed to commit murder tomorrow.

If I had the money I would surely start by buying up television hours to air what is wrong with Islam. It bugs me to no end, when I hear from retired friends that use all their time traveling the world in luxury, when they could do something positive for humanity and the world. As they say, there is a difference between words and actions.

Muhammad not a prophet – Taken from the Internet

1. Muhammad believed he was possessed by a devil when he claimed to have been receiving his religious teachings.

2. Muhammad robbed people much like gangs or drug dealers do to support their evil ways or religion, as some might say like Koresh, the Branch Davidian cult and the Jones Town cult.

3. Muhammad was like any gangster or robber, ruthless towards his victims and towards anyone that opposed him. No one can name anything nice Muhammad did to the people he conquered or villages he ravaged.

4. Muhammad had more wives than what he claimed his revelation suggested including slaves to abuse or rape.

5. Muhammad allowed marriages to six year old girls, which he had one such girl, which he fucked when she became nine-year-old.

6. Muhammad said, "Women are stupid and should be treated like sheep to be beaten as necessary". Women were considered too stupid to become educated. Is this the laws, the stupid British wanted to see imposed on the people, after they helped the Arabs beat off the Turkish invasion?

7. Muhammad was so fucked up in the head claiming his revelation was a mistake from Satan. Sadly, lower life forms, like Muslims, are willing to die for the fuck would say that Muhammad was the last true prophet. It's obvious that all Muslims are pedophiles or want to be one, because they see no wrong with men marrying baby girls, and much of it goes on in secrecy in Muslim society. Should any woman complain they simply murder the girl? Kind of like the Catholic Church and little boys or the Bunga Bunga parties, the Vatican Cardinals were involved in for relaxation.

8. Muhammad was so stupid after decapitating a woman's husband; he then thought that he could rape her, only to be poisoned by the woman when she made him supper. Moreover, here is the best part; she was a Jew. Stick that up your ass Prince of Saudi Arabia and your fucked-up Mullahs, my book that is. Fucking ass-hole ex-presidents that shook the hands of evil ass-holes

like the Saudi and Pakistani leaders or any of those Malaysian and Turkish Muslim douche Bags.

This story in the Quran or the Hadith about Muhammad, it says he had a woman that was breast-feeding a baby torn apart by horses. See Mr. Clinton, Bush and Obama, what idiots you are, all of you ignorant of the truth about the Quran. You are all guilty of the deaths of our soldiers that fought against Muslims.

This for the Negro Colonel Colin Powel, you sir should have known that had the Iraq elite guard been annihilated, while in the open desert, there would not been the inner city skirmishes, which cost the lives of our soldiers. You sir, is a dickhead and owes the families an apology. Promoted for skin-color and not for intelligence in warfare.

Some shit verses from the Quran

Use them when speaking to a Muslims

The Quran gives all children nightmares.

1. If a person speaks in the names of false gods, that person is a false prophet.
Muhammad spoke in the names of false gods.
Therefore, Muhammad was a false prophet.

2. If a person delivers a revelation that doesn't come from God, that person is a false prophet.
Muhammad delivered a revelation that didn't come from God. It says so in the Quran.
Therefore, Muhammad was a false prophet.

By making the people memorize verses study the Quran, the person knows not what he is memorizing, except to understand that much physical harm is metered to those that do not memorize it. What you see written in this book and many similar literatures comes from free thinkers, something that is lacking in the Islamic society. Hence, individuals behaving like zombies as they commit suicide missions. Thanks to stinking American presidents since Eisenhower up to Obama.

3. The Qur'an allows men to beat or murder their wives into subservience. To those on whose part you fear desertion, admonish them, and leave them alone in the sleeping-places and beat them.

According to Muhammad, women lack common sense because their minds are deficient. In other words, women are more like sheep to serve man only or husbands in this case. Have his babies, cook for him; wash his clothes and hundreds of other commands as the husband wishes. He can even kill her and no other Muslim man will say anything regarding the woman's abuse. The husband may also make his wife sleep with strangers just to get on the strangers good side or sell/rent her like a whore to travelers. If she complains, he is free to beat her or murder her at his will much like a goat is murdered for dinner.

Muhammad said women would not be allowed into heaven in the afterlife. So why do so many stupid Muslim women continue to defend Islam or go to Mosques and pray as if, they will be saved after death. It goes to show how well the Islamist have brainwashed their followers.

4. The Qur'an permits Muslims to have sex with their female captives and slaves (i.e. those "whom their right hands possess").

There you go Negros of America and around the world that bend over for Islam. Islam sanctions slavery of Black people and others. Islam is not a Negro religion even though it was started in Africa. It is an Arab religion. Speaking of Arabs, it beats me why Indonesian are Muslims, goes to show how silly some Indonesians are to the world, including the Persians. Any intelligent person that reads the awful Quran would understand that the Quran is nothing but lies, and talks more about repression, and doing evil deeds. It also proves Muhammad the butchers was a mad man, very stupid and evil. How can anyone believe in a douche bag like Muhammad that had 6 to 800 hundred men decapitated in one village? It took his men three days to decapitate them all. What are you followers all STUPID**?**

Verse 9:111 – Muslim's ticket to paradise

"Lo! Allah hath bought from the believers their lives and their wealth because the Garden will be theirs: they shall fight in the way of Allah and shall slay and be slain. It is a promise, which is binding on him in the Torah and the Gospel and the Qur'an. Who fulfilled his covenant better than Allah? Rejoice then in your bargain that ye have made, for that is the supreme triumph."

Islam teaches that if Muslims kill or are murdered in the service of God, i.e. Jihad, they get access paradise where they can fuck forever some 72 virgins. The Quran is nothing more than a book about murder of the innocent and death of your children that follow its teachings. What Muhammad failed to mention was that the virgins were all men with pig like noses causing them to oink during sex. Just like the young men they presently use to dress up like a woman and dance for them before going to bed with the little cross dresser. Shameful Muslims pretending to hate Gay men, while fucking little boys.

5. Kill everyone that is not a Muslim or...

Quran 9:5 "Then, when the sacred months have passed, slay the idolaters wherever ye find them, and take them (captive), and besiege them, and prepare for them each ambush. But if they repent and establish worship and pay the poor-due, then leave their way free. Lo! Allah is Forgiving, Merciful."

This verse is why we often see on the news some dick-head Muslim shooting up a restaurant or movie theatre full of people, or crashing a plane and so on. Kill as many people as you can, what a psychopath Muhammad must have been. The people must convert to either Islam, or pay the tax and can even be murdered at will. How can anyone with some common sense ever believe that a God wants you to murder his creations? How stupid do you have to be to believe in the Quran or a psychopath as your savior? Congress must be brain dead to not see Islam as a cult religion of evil.

6. Pay tax or die

Quran 9:29:

"Fight against such of those who have been given the Scripture as believe not in Allah nor the Last Day, and forbid not that which Allah hath forbidden by His messenger, and follow not the Religion of Truth, until they pay the tribute readily, being brought low."

This is where the Butcher Mohammad tells his followers that the conquered should be humiliated and made to pay a tax or to be murdered. This surely is more like the teaching of Hitler where he was ordering the rounding up of anyone that was not German. Either Hitler had them murdered or they were made to work for the Nazi Party making weapons, to murder more victims. It is shameful for Muslims to believe in the Quran.

7. Unimaginable cruelty

Quran 5:32-33

"We decreed for the Children of Israel that whosoever killeth a human being for other than manslaughter or corruption in the earth, it shall be as if he had murdered all mankind, and whoso saveth the life of one, it shall be as if he had saved the life of all mankind."

In order to portray Islam as a peaceful religion, Muslim taqiyah tacticians, including President Obama, will always quote verse 5:32, as he did in Cairo. Taqiyah means to protect or as some might see it as a white lie, in this case lying about the evils of Islam. 5:32 is nothing more than mass genocide of the innocent. The ass Obama just indicated that it was OK for the mass murdered of Americans by quoting this stinking lying Quranic verse. As expected from a Negro president of low IQ.

Verse 5:33 says:

"The only reward of those who make war upon Allah and His messenger and strive after corruption in the land will be that they will be murdered or crucified, or have

their hands and feet on alternate sides cut off, or will be expelled out of the land. Such will be their degradation in the world, and in the Hereafter theirs will be an awful doom;"

What happened President Obama to this verse, you stupid person. Chicken shit for a president to cower away from the rest of the evil words from the Quran. Not so peaceful for you Obama is that why you purposely avoided speaking about it? Every word is nothing but cruel and evil behavior sanctioned by the Muslims and by President Clinton (Whore), the Bush presidents and President Obama. How dare any of the Presidents claim that Islam is a peaceful religion, there is nothing religious about Islam. The mass murders committed around the world are all carried out by Muslims, forced to be brainwashed by repressive governments that remain in power by stupid American presidents ever since the First World War I. Yep, that's you Eisenhower too.

I can see and understand that when any of the dignitaries from Washington or from Europe visit one of the Muslim run countries, they are often greeted as if everything is beautiful and peaceful and everyone seems happy, because that is all they get to see. That's what you would expect when visiting just about any family home, that is doing well or working in America. However, that is not what is truly happening to the majority of the population in these Muslim repressed countries. While rich Saudis are free to party at discoes, drink liquor, do drugs and purchase prostitutes, the rest of the Muslim population are made to memorize the Quran, and be punished for any insurrections. Insurrections like reading the Bible or a book titled, "The People Verses Muhammad". The rich family girls can talk to another man at these parties, but a woman from an average worker or poor family could get her face disfigured from an acid attack, or the girl could receive 100 lashes or even murder. It all depends on how much the parents or the husband feels the woman has dishonored the family. These barbaric Muslim behaviors are what American presidents have been lying about; telling Americans Islam is a peaceful religion. What is occurring in the Muslim world is Muslims throwing stones when every one of them is a sinner.

8. Pedophilia Muslims

Quran 65:4:

"And those of your women as have passed the age of monthly courses, for them the 'Iddah (prescribed divorce period), if you have doubts (about their periods), is three months, and for those who have no courses [(i.e. they are still immature) their 'Iddah (prescribed period) is three months likewise, except in case of death]. And for those who are pregnant (whether they are divorced or their husbands are dead), their

'Iddah (prescribed period) is until they deliver (their burdens) (give birth) and whosoever fears Allah and keeps his duty to Him, He will make his matter easy for him."

What better way to justify molesting little boys and girl while they are still babies than to seek the OK from a religious text. You can thank the presidents of the United States for all of them stating that Islam is a peaceful religion. It's expected since many of the presidents no doubt in my mind received millions to support the election and re-elections. And shame on you losers that voted for Hillary Clinton, we know for sure she was receiving hundreds of thousands of dollars from the Arabs. The very same animals like the Saudi that were funding ISIS the biggest terrorist of all.

This verse 65:4 condones sex with pre-pubescent baby girls as the evil Muhammad did with his nine-year-old wife. Read it and reap evil Obama and all Americans assisting Muslims.

The Quran I'll have you know also blesses incest, it says, if you cannot help yourself it's okay. This is why a large portion of the Muslim population has both physical and mental defects amongst its people. Once they are stupid, it does not take much to keep them down, dahhh.

I might add that a study found that red heads (ginger people) are more likely to convert to Islam. This was shown on a television documentary and it had to do when people low self-esteem. As a Muslim they could feel belonged and allowed to vent via committing murder in the name of Allah.

9. Okay to have slaves and to rape them whenever.

Verse 33.50 says:

"O Prophet! surely We have made lawful to you your wives whom you have given their dowries, and those [slaves] whom your right hand possesses out of those whom Allah has given to you as prisoners of war, and the daughters of your paternal uncles and the daughters of your paternal aunts, and the daughters of your maternal uncles and the daughters of your maternal aunts who fled with you; and a believing woman if she gave herself to the Prophet, if the Prophet desired to marry her – specially for you, not for the (rest of) believers; We know what We have ordained for them concerning their wives and those whom their right hands possess in order that no blame may attach to you; and Allah is Forgiving, Merciful".

This verse should have been a slap in the face of President Obama, and his Black wife, I hear she is a man. Yeah, my mother saw she was a man when Obama was first elected president, her sister in Italy noticed it too (see the truth on YouTube). My Italian mother called me one day and said, "She looka like a man."

Slavery is OK Obama, really. Goes to show you how incompetent our Negro president is or was. The multiple wives Muhammad the psycho butcher had was way more than what the evil Quran indicated you could have. He simple wanted to fuck whomever he wanted and changed the rules as if fit him. The douche bag even took his son's wife to fuck. This is a peaceful religion Mr. Obama. Come-on Congress and amend the freedom of religion clause. After all the Aztec was a religion too so why can't they practice human sacrifices. Just think if Aztec were allowed to practice per our First Amendment along the Mexico and US borders, you would not need a fence. Anyone crossing is fair game for the Aztec to capture, just kidding. What is the difference between the Aztec and Muslims murdering using suicide bombers? Muslims are murdering the innocent based on their Quran, which states in two places to kill the unbelievers. I know nothing will change until one of you asses in Congress has one of your own family members murdered by a Muslim. Then we will hear the same garbage spewing from the White House, "It was not foreseen, or relax people, just a lone suicide."

10. Physical assaults on your wife are OK. You would be hard pressed to find a Mullah that would sympathize with the woman.

Quran 4:34:

"Men are the maintainers of women because Allah has made some of them to excel others and because they spend out of their property; the good women are therefore obedient, guarding the unseen as Allah has guarded; and (as to) those on whose part you fear desertion, admonish them, and leave them alone in the sleeping-places and beat them; then if they obey you, do not seek a way against them; surely Allah is High, Great."

Ass-hole Muslims begin beating and repressing little girls at the age of five so they get used to being repressed. This was seen in Afghanistan when our troops were there to liberate the people from the Taliban. Little girls were seen being kick by her much younger brother to get back in the house. Women are often forced to remain indoors, never to again enjoy the outdoors alone. A man has to be with a woman 24/7 or she will receive lashings in public, and possibly is even murdered in public, as a warning to other girls. Goats and sheep do not know what's coming next, but young girls must live with threats daily. This is the kind of world our Stinking evil Obama claims is peaceful and why not he's Muslim no matter what he claims. His parents or father was one, therefore, like that other evil Negro, Michael Vick (Philly football player) the dog torturer. Obama assumes since his Dad was a wife beater I presume he feels it's Ok as was Vick to justify torturing his dogs... Women are considered property and as such not allowed to make any decisions. Any time the husband wants to screw her any way he wants she must submit, no different from the way Arab sheep herders jumped on their flock of sheep. Sheep don't answer back they go where they are herded and that's the way Muslim men feel they can treat a woman. How many time have we read or saw in the news a woman is disfigured by her Muslim husband. Is this the peaceful Islam Obama speaks of? How many disfigured faces have Obama fixed or paid for fixing in his life time?

11. Like all gang thieves, Muhammad the butcher takes a cut of the loot.

Quran 8:41:

"And know that out of all the booty that ye may acquire (in war), ***a fifth share is assigned to Allah, - and to the Messenger****, and to near relatives, orphans, the needy, and the wayfarer, - if ye do believe in Allah and in the revelation We sent down to Our servant on the Day of Testing, - the Day of the meeting of the two forces. For Allah hath power over all things."*

Can you imagine an ass-hole like Obama stating the Islam is peaceful, when in this verse, it says to go ahead and steal but make sure that I get my cut because Allah said I'm entitled to it. Can you believe that a religious book condones theft and slaughter? Hey, Congress of the United States/Washington D.C., get your turd-covered head out of your asses and read the Quran. No wonder thousands of people around the world are dying from murders committed by brainwashing Mullahs. To remain silent indicates that you condone the wholesale murder of innocent people while hiding behind political correctness. Shame on Washington for bending over for the few evil ones in our society. In my book, "NAVSEA," I foretold the possibility of such an attack as occurred at Fort Hood. And yet NAVSEA continues to deny that Muslim working within the Navy are safe. There is no difference between a Klansman and a Muslim wearing a Turban, both are racist and out to rule the world.

12. Allah is a Dick Head of the most evil, the world has ever witnessed. The Devils henchman disguised as a prophet.

Quran 24:2:

"The woman and the man guilty of adultery or fornication, -- flog each of them with a hundred stripes: Let not compassion move you in their case, in a matter prescribed by God, if ye believe in God and the Last Day: and let a party of the Believers witness their punishment."

This shit verse from the Butcher Muhammad says to whip them having adultery to 100 lashes in public. Nevertheless, at the same time it's OK to fuck your slaves or captives all you want. Allah says this shit is OK by him. One hundred lashes? Are you fucking kidding me, that can kill a person in the most horrible way to die, and you butt-hole Muslims say this is good, really?

13. Torture, Slavery, Decapitation and blinding all that go against the Quran.

There is over three thousand other teachings in the stinking Quran about metering out torture, slavery and murder.

TORTURE

Quran 22:19-22: "*fight and slay the Pagans, seize them, beleaguer them, and lie in wait for them in every stratagem" "for them (the unbelievers) garments of fire shall be cut and there shall be poured over their heads boiling water whereby whatever is in their bowels and skin shall be dissolved and they will be punished with hooked iron rods*"

SLAVERY

Quran 2.178: "*O you who believe! retaliation is prescribed for you in the matter of the slain, the free for the free, and the slave for the slave, and the female for the female, but if any remission is made to any one by his (aggrieved) brother, then prosecution (for the bloodwit) should be made according to usage, and payment should be made to him in a good manner; this is an alleviation from your Lord and a mercy; so whoever exceeds the limit after this he shall have a painful chastisement.*"

If you kill one of my slaves, I get to kill one of yours. Hey, Saudi Arabia you piece of shit for a country is this what you, force your followers to memorize. Saudi are like Pit Bull dogs in that they breed like them in supported Madrasahs to the point where these mad dogs are coming home to bite their masters after discovering the shelters are overrun with unwanted dangerous dogs, hence, all the into fighting in the Middle East.

How stupid do you have to be as a Negro, who believes in Islam? Muslims would have enslaved your ass, as many of them still do today. Islam is an Arab religion and had nothing to do with Negros. Arabs in fact enslaved Negros to sell to the Europeans and the Americas. That is how Arabs made money by selling your ass. Muhammad you fools should know, had many slaves and you Negros complain about slavery in Americas past as if it explains all your troubles? Go visit any Muslim country and you will still find Muslims enslaving Negros in some form. The US calls it racism as if slavery does not exist in those repressive countries. Arabs enslave Phillipinoes, Indians and just about anyone, they can get their sticky goat-smelling fingers on.

By the way, Black People, when I was 14 living in Montana, I was bucking hay bales, from six in the morning until six in the evening. In North Dakota, I was shoveling snow in 30 degrees below zero temperatures, and in the summer at 110 degrees, I hoeing sugar beets on quarter mile long fields at $1.45 per row, with Mexican laborers, and we all drank out of the same water container using the same ladle. Some of the Mexicans looked as if they had leprosy. When we moved to New Jersey, I was picking peaches and tomatoes at 25 cents a basket with Mexican and Puerto Rican farm labors. I was working so I could buy my school clothes, shoes and school lunch, and not once did I see a Black ass person in any of those fields. The world is getting tired of you people wining whenever you do something bad, and then you want to blame it all on slavery. Get a life and earn a living like everyone else, Muslims not included.

CRUELTY

Quran 5:38: "*Cut off the hands of thieves, whether they are male or female, as punishment for what they have done-a deterrent from God: God is almighty and wise." 39 "But if anyone repents after his wrongdoing and makes amends, God will accept his repentance: God is most forgiving and merciful.*"

Muslims around the world do not follow the verse in all cases when someone has stolen something. It is as if they always have to send a message to the public watching, as some young boy gets his hand cut off or crushed under the wheel of a heavy truck. Muslims relish the spectacle of seeing a person be tortured as a way of venting anger, which is ingrained into their sole since childhood from being forced to memorize the Quran. Memorizing is not the same as understanding what is read. Only the free world is capable of doing so. It is the very essence of this book, and everything the public is witnessing on the internet, television and through public dialog regarding the evils of the Quran.

EYE FOR EYE

Quran 5:45: "*And We prescribed for them therein: The life for the life, and the eye for the eye, and the nose for the nose, and the ear for the ear, and the tooth for the tooth, and for wounds retaliation. But whoso forgoeth it (in the way of charity) it shall be expiation for him. Whoso judgeth not by that which Allah hath revealed such as wrong-doers.*"

Muhammad knew a man, so the story goes; this man stole a horse and he was later apprehended by Muhammad's warriors. Muhammad had both his hands and feet cut off, and had him blinded. Then Muhammad left him to die in the desert. This is the shit person you Muslims say is a prophet, if you still do consider yourself an idiot and very evil.

BEHEADING

Quran 8.12: "*Remember thy Lord inspired the angels (with the message): "I am with you: give firmness to the Believers: I will instill terror into the hearts of the Unbelievers: smite ye above their necks and smite all their finger-tips off them.*"

The evil book of the Quran mentions decapitations seventy-five times. You still believe the Quran is peaceful - shameful Obama, Bush and Clinton presidents.

The following is from James M. Arlandson

In AD 627, Muhammad committed an atrocity against the last remaining major tribe of Jews in Medina: the Qurayza. He beheaded the men and the pubescent boys and enslaved the women and children.

Sources: Ibn Ishaq, pp. 463-64; Tabari vol. 8, p. 34.

The sentence: Death by decapitation for 300-600 men and pubescent boys, and enslavement for the women and children. Ibn Ishaq says that the number may have been as high as 800-900.

Muhammad was wise enough to have six clans execute two Jews each in order to stop any blood feuds. The rest of the executions were probably carried out by Muhammad's fellow Emigrants from Mecca, as the heads and bodies were dragged into trenches in the business district of Medina.

Source: Watt, *Muhammad: Prophet and Statesman*, p. 174

How did the executioners decide on which boy to slaughter or leave alive? This hadith gives the obvious answer.

Narrated Atiyyah al-Qurazi: I was among the captives of Banu [tribe] Qurayzah. They (the Companions) examined us, those who had begun to grow hair (pubes) were murdered, and those who had not were not murdered. I was among those who had not grown hair. (Abu Dawud; see Ibn Ishaq, p. 466)

This truth about Muhammad should be the corner stone why Islam is bad and not a religion at all. Stop harping on pedophile, which was common during Muhammad's time and it was even common in the US. In America today, there exist ass-holes in Utah (multiple wives on welfare) and in the Carolinas where children are auctioned off to the highest bidders for marriage. It is all done in secrecy and no one in Washington has the balls to put an end to it. Most of these pedophiles are Irish by the way.

SLAUGHTERING

Quran-8:67: "*It is not for any prophet to have captives until he hath made slaughter in the land. Ye desire the lure of this world and Allah desireth (for you) the Hereafter, and Allah is Mighty, Wise.*" (Allah insisting Prophet to kill all the prisoners, and should not keep any surrendered prisoners alive until He (Prophet) occupied entire Arabia.)

Jihadist will always exist as long as they receive sustenance from the Quran with US and European support. *Lawrence Lueder 2017*

Congress should act to dissolve Islam

There you go Congress of the United States. Stop being a bunch of douche bags and fix the first amendment:

"Congress shall make no law respecting an establishment of religion, or prohibiting the free exercise thereof; or abridging the freedom of speech, or of the press; or the right of the people peaceably to assemble, and to petition the government for a redress of grievances."

What is wrong by adding the sentence that says after *thereof,* **except one that is repressive (expand to define it), evil, does not abide by governing laws, or is involved in politics (define involved)**? What is wrong with that? How many more have to die before Congress finally makes sense to the world. The United States was the leader for the world to follow and it is the main reason why so many other countries allow Islam to exist, simply because many of them would lose trade or more. Other countries are made to mimic the United States. All religions need limits, which is lacking in the Constitution.

What some of you, ass-holes, in Washington fail to realize is that all of you are violating the First Amendment, by arming one religion over all others in the Middle East. You are favoring the evil cult of Islam and you all need to be stopped. No other religion in the world has been armed to the teeth as our American presidents have been doing for decades for countries like Saudi Arabia, Pakistan and Malaysia. Malaysian are the very essences of the killings that have been going on in the Philippines, if didn't know. And yet, our presidents keeps arming the Malaysians. So, while our leaders tell Americans to disarm they freely arm terrorist like the Saudi and the Pakistani. The Saudi, brainwash children, to become suicide bombers, in exchange for food and shelter in Madrasahs Schools. You ex-presidents shamed the most respected country in the world, the U.S... May God have mercy on your stinking carcass. All you stinking ex-presidents knew this, and yet continued to arm the very butchers of a cult religion.

By arming the stinking Saudi, you ex-presidents violated the slavery laws, which are practiced by the Saudi as of 2017. FUCK YOU, OBAMA for arming the Saudi with 15 Billion dollars in arms, just before leaving office.

What made the US powerful was diversity and tons of resources. That was then, ever since 1965, the US opened its borders to the world because of a few ass-hole minorities that would not shut the fuck up, they kept protesting that Africans and Arabs/Muslims were good for the economy. We now know we have a problem. Yes, America benefitted some; however, America is slowly becoming a welfare country supporting more people, which are non-productive. They have become like an invasive species that breeds 10 fold over all others.

My mother is from Sicily and I know that she is impossible to teach how computers work. I cannot even get her to use a credit card, it's simply too complex for her mind to comprehend. I had/have brothers that are and were like that. Moreover, while working for the Navy I knew of workers that were just as illiterate when it came to using a computer or anything that was technical in nature. And it is this, that America is becoming, because people with lower intelligence tend to breed more like wildlife with no concept of tomorrow or how they will feed that extra mouth. The more intelligent people seem to understand that children require a lot, and this is the reason that the creative population is going down, while the minorities are exploding, the pyramid effect. Who will support them tomorrow? And yes, I know some whites are not as intelligent, I mentioned my mother and some do breed more than they can support. So while Congress waits for things to get out of hand, the forced teaching of the Quran creates more illiterates and potentially dangerous followers.

A wall to keep out immigrants seems okay for Congress to approve. The wall is there to keep hard working farm workers out while at the same time, Congress does nothing to stop the destruction and deaths that are constantly occurring from Muslims. Where is the wall to stop the teachings of Islam? If a school in America were to teach children about white supremacy or white power or even Black Power, you could bet that Congress would react immediately to put an end to it. Islam is a cult and nothing else; it wages war, stores weapons in Mosques and often teaches followers how to make explosives and to multiply (breed) using the free world's welfare system.

There are many undercover investigations done in Europe, which show how deceptive and evil the Mullahs from these mosques truly are. They distort the truth about other religions in order to boost their standing above all. What they say in public is not, what they say and do, behind an exclusionary guarding system. When you teach religion in secrecy, it can only mean one thing and that is there will be trouble to come.

Everyday Congress does not react because of political correctness innocent lives are lost. If there is a God, may he have mercy on those that continue to put their head in the sand? A religion cannot be both peaceful and evil at the same time to be considered a legitimate religion. What there presently exist in Islam is both good and evil, which explains why you see some individuals peacefully praying in a Mosque, while others use the Quran to justify torture, slavery and murder. We should not be waking up to read, that another innocent person was murdered by a Muslim, claiming he had a right to murder because it says he can per the Quran. Wake up Congress!

Islam personifies Man's inhumanity towards his fellow man, and especially towards woman's rights. Why are the representatives in Washington so blind of Muslims behaving badly in a country that is supposed to have the best democracy in the world? Only Muslims commit murder of anyone who question the Quran or draws a cartoon of the butcher Muhammad. And they remain silent when Muslins burn school girls alive. How can we as Americans continue to allow Muslims to intimidate people of the free world?

If Washington reps are afraid to make changes or pass laws to limit repressive religious practices then perhaps there are methods to make changes come about. It's called Advertising/propaganda, however, in this situations it's the truth about the evils of Islam and that Muhammad was never any kind of prophet. So long as Washington continues to pretend that, there is no enemies with-in our borders and nearby, we are doomed for another major attack by some nut job Muslim. I hope that should some person that has lost a loved one to some Muslim attack that that person files a major suit against the Politically correct Washington representatives and files charges against the president of the United States for treason. The world has had enough of the phony cover up that Washington perpetuates which allows Muslims to justify their evil mannerism. Cover up by Washington gives credence to the evil teaching of the Quran. And it demonstrates Washington's unwillingness to protect its citizens from an invasion the world is about to witness as a surprise attack like all other Islamic have been in the past and every day.

Muslims do nothing to stop some of their own showing videos of innocent people being decapitated, the stoning of women or the public whipping and other evils. And what about that cute images of a boy roughly five years old wearing a suicide vest, care to label Islam peaceful Mr. idiot Obama, or Bush.

The longer Washington drags it feet the more likely the sane portion of society will begin to form marches to Washington D.C. The sore is festering Washington. More uneducated immigrants equates to a huge influx of welfare recipients, including their way into their retirement age thereby reducing funds available to existing wage earners. The whole intelligence pyramid scale of America flattens according to the number on immigrants.

The Crusaders and Witch Burning Justification.

Stupid people that defend Islam are those that will say something like, "What about the Crusaders or the Witch burning or the inquisitions for justifying Islam's existence. Listen mud heads, Jesus was none of those, he never murdered or stole or raped anyone to send his message of love. Neither did any of the other religious founders except for the butcher Muhammad. Muhammad murdered thousands, he stole from his captives, enslaved people and raped. That is the difference between Jesus and Muhammad. The Crusaders, Witch burners or the Vatican Cardinal Bunga-Bunga parties were all common people with a sick demented mind regarding religion. Muslims on the other hand, continue to this day raping, stealing murdering and enslaving in the name of their evil founder, the Butcher Muhammad. I venture to guess that Muhammad was Satan in disguise.

There is nothing, which proves Islam is a religion, it is a cult if anything. Allah in Jewish is tree, the stone they worship around in Mecca; belonged to idol worshippers before Muhammad had the worshippers all murdered and claimed the stone Muslim. All the good portions of the Quran were taken from the Bible or the Torah word for word, proving that the Quran is a fake. Even Mecca is in the wrong location according to the Quran, the original city was in Petra, Jordan.

Everywhere you see Jesus mentioned in the Bible, the word love is associated with his name. In the Quran whenever Muhammad name is mentioned death, and murder is associated with it.

General James Mattis

General. James Mattis, known to his troops as "Mad Dog Mattis,"

This General says what true Americans what them to hear, not the pussy stuff that spewed out of the Obama filthy face, "Islam is peaceful". Obamas ass would have been running if Mattis had his way, and Obama would have been charged with treason for aiding the terrorist like Pakistan and Saudi Arabia.

Here are just a few of General Matis speech.

"The first time you blow someone away is not an insignificant event. That said there are some assholes in the world that just need to be shot."

Yeah like the Saudi leadership for funding forced Islamic reading and for supporting terrorist groups like ISIS, and repressive Pakistani leaders that keep murdered Indians with no repercussions. Pakistani are two-face taking American dollars while pretending to fight terrorist.

"Find the enemy that wants to end this experiment (in American democracy) and kill every one of them until they're so sick of the murdered that they leave us and our freedoms intact."

We have yet to slap the biggest supporter of terrorism, the Saudi Government. Instead, our shit for brains presidents from the Bushes, to Clinton and to Obama all provided billions in arms to people that were torturing and committing murder overall. Islam is nothing more than another name for **Religious Revolutionaries**.

When America tries to stop drugs from getting into our country it goes after the head of the drug trade. Why ain't we going after the Mullahs that force the teaching of the Quran?

"You cannot allow any of your people to avoid the brutal facts. If they start living in a dream world, it's going to be bad."

Yeah, this means that Ass-hole like Obama should or should have stopped lying to the American people about the peaceful Muslims. Right this way in case this is published after Obama leaves office so the place can be fumigated.

"You go into Afghanistan; you got guys who slap women around for five years because they didn't wear a veil. You know, guys like that ain't got no manhood left anyway. So it's a hell of a lot of fun to shoot them. Actually, it's quite fun to fight them, you know. It's a hell of a hoot. It's fun to shoot some people. I'll be right up there with you. I like brawling."

Mattis is telling idiot Obama that Afghan men need to be taught a lesson. So far it's been the Muslims that are teaching Americans the they can get away with murder, death means nothing to them, they will be receiving 72 virgins all cross-dressers with piglet noses. Muslims easily wrote the book, *How to commit murder and get away with it*. Murder is justified in their Quran. Will the brain dead in Congress tell me what cult in America is allowed to preach, death to innocent people like it does in the Quran.

Like it or not Islam is quietly stifling America with its religious cult demands. So while Mosques are allowed to exist in America, no other religious building is allowed in their Islamic country of origin. What happened to tit for tack? Why is America bending for a repressive ideology? Must there be another mass murdered before America does something? When Muslims attack, it will always be said that, he was a lone attacker.

Islam is the torture of the brainwashed and repressed people that has no place in the free world. To allow its existence is to allow a cancer to grow. Lawrence Lueder 2017.

Brave Honorable Enlighteners

Bridget Gabriel

Bridget Gabriel you can watch her videos on YouTube. What a great speaker about how Muslims plan to take over America and the rest of the world. Please, take the time to watch her video**, They must be stopped**.

David Wood

This person is on the money, I learned a lot from him. He is line and verse in the Quran where he details everything that is ridiculous about the Quran, that it's fake, that it is copied from the Bible, and that it constantly speaks about murdering, raping and slavery. He even shows where Muhammad is a nut case and much more. Watch him too on YouTube. The are other proofs on the internet that show Muhammad's Quran was a fake taken from similar verses in the Bible and he adds his own evil twist to it.

Simon Rushdie

Who can forget this person, who seems to have started it all with his book, *Satanic Verses*?

Many other contributors too numerous to name them all see them on the internet.

Thomas Jefferson

According to historical records, Jefferson, in the 1786, wrote against Islam in America. What happened to that portion of our Constitution?

Islamic Terrorism around the World

No Thanks to American Presidents for labeling Islam Peaceful

The following is a Chronological List of Islamic Terrorist Attacks, 1968 – Now, which changes daily thanks to the evil verses of the Quran. Islam takes over where the NAZI PARTY Left off, make no mistake, only this time all the free people will be imprisoned, enslaved or murdered. Welcome to the truths about Islam Mr. President.

Take notice as you go over the list, the frequency of the attacks increases each year. On YouTube there is a videos showing what occurs as the number of Muslims increases over time. It's like placing a frog in warm water and slowly turning up the heat until the frog is dead. The same thing is happening to Europe and North America. Already Muslims are demanding halal foods and places of worship at airports and malls, etc. They are enforcing these changes via the First Amendment. Muslims on airlines are demanding that they **not** be seated next to a women and **refuse** to be served by women stewards. I ask congress, "How much Muslim SHIT must free Americans have to put up with before they take up arms to make changes happen, changes not for the few but the many?" All over Europe, China and places like Japan the people are fighting back Islam. What were once beautiful cultures are being destroyed by Islamic ideology. Italy, France, London and places like Japan are becoming too dangerous for tourist, and the same is happening in America wherever Muslims are residing.

The Short List of Evil Islamic Deeds follows:

1968

June 5 - U.S. presidential candidate Robert Kennedy murdered by Palestinian Sirhan Sirhan, in Los Angeles, which causes further terrorist attacks, as Arab terrorist groups demanded his release.

1969

Feb. 18 - Boeing 707 attacked at Zurich, Switzerland, murdered the pilot and three passengers.

Aug. 29 - TWA 707 hijacked from Rome to Damascus, released with only wounded.

Nov. 27- EL AL office in Athens, Greece attacked. Innocent bystanders murdered.

1970

Feb. 21 - Swiss airliner blown up over Switzerland, murdered all 47 people on board.

Feb. 23 - PLO terrorists open fire on a busload of Christian pilgrims murdered 1 and wounding 2 Americans.

April 21- Bomb explodes aboard a Philippines airliner. All 36 aboard are murdered.

Sept. 6 - "Skyjack Sunday" in Jordan. Three planes (TWA, Swissair, and Pan Am) on route to the U.S. hijacked 400+ hostages, planes blown up in Jordan, Governments agreed to PFLP's demands, released terrorists from jails and hostages released. Popular Front for the Liberation of Palestine (PFLP)

Sept. 14 - The PFLP hijacked TWA flight to Ammon, 4 Americans injured.

1971

Nov. 28 - Jordanian Prime Minister Tal murdered by terrorists at the Sheraton Hotel in Cairo, Egypt.

Dec. 1 - Jordanian ambassador to London, England is shot by hit squad.

1972

Jan. 26 - Bomb explodes on a Yugoslav plane murdered all but one passenger.

May 30 - Ben Gurion Airport, Israel, attack murdered 26, and wounded 78 U.S. citizens from Puerto Rico.

Sept. 5 - Palestinian terrorists seize 11 athletes in the Olympic Village in Munich, Germany, 9 hostages and 5 terrorists murdered, plus David Berger from Cleveland.

1973

March 2 - Khartoum, Sudan. Cleo Noel, Jr., U.S. ambassador, and George C. Moore, U.S. diplomat, were held hostage and then murdered by terrorists at the U.S. Embassy.

Aug. 5 - Suicide squad attacks Athens airport, Greece, murdered 3 civilians and injuring 55.

Dec. 17 - Bomb explodes at Pan Am office at Rome, Italy murdered 32 and injuring 50+. The terrorists take seven Italian police officers hostage and hijack an aircraft to Athens, Greece, murdering one of them.

1974

March 1 - Diplomats taken hostage from Saudi Arabian Embassy in Khartoum, Sudan, 2 that are murdered are Americans.

April 11 - Kiryat Shmona Massacre at an apartment building murdering 18 people, 9 were children.

Sept. 8 - Athens, Greece. TWA Flight 841 exploded from bomb in cargo hold, all 88 passengers murdered, including 32-year-old Steven Lowe, an American citizen.

Nov. 23 - British DC-10 hijacked at Dubai, UAE, flown to Tunisia where a German passenger was murdered.

1975

Jan. 19 - Arab terrorists attack Orly airport, Paris, France, seizing 10 hostages from a bathroom. French provided the terrorists with a plane to fly them to safety in Baghdad, Iraq.

Sept. 30 - Hungarian airplane explodes murdering all 64 persons on board.

Dec. 21 - Carlos "The Jackal" holds 11 oil ministers and 59 civilians' hostage during the OPEC meeting in Vienna, Austria. Flew to Algeria, got $300,000,000 in ransom money, Carlos and his Popular Front for the Liberation of Palestine terrorists escape.

1976

Jan. 1 - 82 innocent travelers are murdered aboard a Lebanese plane.

June 27 - Air France airliner hijacked and forced to fly to Uganda. Some 258 passengers and crew are held hostage. Three passengers were murdered. July 4th, Israeli commandos rescue the remaining hostages.

Aug. 11 - Terrorists attack Istanbul airport, Turkey, murdered 4 civilians (1 from U.S.) and injuring 20.

Dec. 4 - Terrorists occupied the Indonesian Embassy in The Hague, Netherlands, 1 official murdered.

Dec. 14 - Passenger train hijacked and passengers were kept hostage, 3 were murdered.

1977

Jan. 1 - F.E. Melov U.S. ambassador to Lebanon, and Robert O.Waring, the U.S. economic counselor, kidnapped and later murdered in Beirut.

Oct. 13 - Palestinian terrorists hijack a Lufthansa Flight 181 Boeing 737 and order it to fly around a number of Middle East destinations for four days; pilot is murdered by the terrorists, 90 hostages rescued.

1978

March 11 - Gail Rubin, niece of U.S. Senator Ribicoff, among 38 people shot to death by terrorists on a beach near Tel Aviv.

June 2 - A bomb kills two people at the CHOGM meeting in Sydney Australia.

1979

July 29 - Terrorist bombs two railway stations in Madrid, murdering seven.

Nov. 4 - Terrorists seized the U.S. Embassy in Tehran and took 66 American diplomats hostage. Thirteen freed, but the remaining 53 were held until their release on January 20, 1981 - 444 days - at the inauguration of President Ronald Reagan.

1980

April 30 - Terrorists took over the Iranian Embassy in London, holding 26 hostages, two of whom were murdered on May 5th after being tortured. Much of the embassy was destroyed by fire.

1981

April 19 - 13 people murdered, 177 injured in a terrorist attack in Davao Philippines.

May 13 - Pope John Paul II seriously wounded in assassination attempt in Rome, Italy, by terrorist Mehmet Ali Agca.

Oct. 6 - Egyptian President Anwar Sadat machine gunned dead by Islamic Jihad in Cairo for working for peace. Seven others murdered, 28 wounded. The assassins are later executed.

1982

Beginning of the 8 years of terrorism in Lebanon by Muslims, all thanks to Washington DC for sanctioning Islam as religion of peace.

July 19 - David Dodge, President of the American University in Beirut kidnapped, spends one year in captivity.

Aug. 19 - Two American citizens, Anne Van Zanten and Grace Cutler, were murdered along with six others when the PLO bombed a kosher restaurant in Paris, France.

Sept. 14 - Lebanon's President Gemayel and 26 others assassinated by a massive car bomb in Beirut.

1983

Mar. 16 - five Marines wounded in hand grenade attack on Beirut International Airport.

April 18 - CIA's Middle East Director, and 83 others are murdered, 120 injured in truck bomb on the US Embassy in Lebanon.

Sept. 29 - Gulf Air Flight 771 is bombed, explodes murdering all 166 aboard.

Oct. 23 - Simultaneous suicide truck bombs in Lebanon: first crashed into lobby of US Marine Corps Headquarters, 241 Marines murdered, 82 seriously injured - and second was the French compound murdering 58 paratroopers.

Dec. 12 - US Embassy in Kuwait targeted to destroy the building with a truck bomb; attack foiled by guards and the device murdered five people and injured 80.

1984

Jan. 18 - Malcolm Kerr, President of the American University of Beirut, was murdered by two Hezbollah gunmen.

Mar. 8 - Rev. Weir and wife kidnapped in Lebanon and held for 16 months.

Mar. 9 - Car bomb murders 80 (22 Americans) and wounds more than 200 civilians when it drove past the checkpoint at the U.S. Embassy in Awkar.

Mar. 16 - Hezbollah kidnapped, tortured and murdered William Buckley, an officer at the U.S. Embassy in Beirut.

Apr. 12 - Hezbollah bombed restaurant adjacent to US Air Force base in Tarragon Spain, 18 service members murdered and 83 Americans wounded.

Sept. 20- US embassy in the Beirut is bombed - two service members and 23 employees are murdered, 21 Americans injured including the U.S. and British Ambassadors. 50+ Lebanese were injured.

Dec. 4 - Terrorists hijacked Kuwait Airlines Flight 221 and demanded the release from Kuwaiti jails of some members, serving sentences for attacks on French and American targets. Two Americans murdered.

1985

March 16 - US journalist Terry Anderson kidnapped in Lebanon, finally released in Dec. 1991 - 6 years later.

April 5 - Bomb explodes outside Hezbollah headquarters in Beirut murdering 80 people.

April 12 - Bombing of U.S. soldier's favorite restaurant in Madrid murdering 18, and injuring 82.

June 14 - TWA Boeing 727, Flight 847 hijacked on route to Rome, 8 crew and 145 passengers were held for 17 days, U.S. Navy diver was murdered. After being flown twice to Algiers, the hostages were released after the US pressured to release 435 Lebanese and Palestinian prisoners.

Sept. 30 - Four Soviet diplomats kidnapped in Lebanon, 1 murdered but other three released unharmed after a relative of the terrorist leader was kidnapped and murdered by the Soviet KGB.

Oct. 7 - Terrorists seize the Italian cruise liner, Achille Lauro, during a cruise in the Mediterranean, taking more than 700 people hostage for 3 days. Disabled U.S. citizen, Leon Klinghoffer, was murdered in front of other hostages by throwing him in the ocean, before the Egyptian Government offered the terrorists safe haven in return for the hostages' freedom.

Nov. 23 - 98 passengers and crew of an Egypt air Flight 648 are held hostage by Palestinian terrorists in Malta. Five passengers shot, 2 died, later 57 additional passengers murdered when the terrorists set off explosives in the aircraft.

Dec. 27 - Suicide grenade and gun attacks in passenger terminals at Rome and Vienna, Italy airports results in 16 people being murdered plus 5 Americans and more than 100 civilians injured.

1986

March 30-April 2nd - A bomb exploded on a TWA flight 840 from Rome as it approached Athens airport. The attack murdered four U.S. citizens who were sucked through a hole made by the blast, one infant, and 9 injured, although the plane safely landed.

April 6 - An explosion at the "La Belle" nightclub in Berlin, U.S. soldiers' hangout was bombed, murdered 3 and injuring 230 people, including 79 U.S. soldiers.

Sept. 5 - Pan Am Boeing 747 Flight 73 on route to Frankfurt and on to New York hijacked by Palestinian terrorists, with 379 passengers, including 89 Americans, 22 hostages were murdered, 127 wounded.

Sept. 9 - Hezbollah kidnapped Frank Reed, President of American University in Beirut, and held for 44 months, and Joseph Cicippio, and Edward Tracy who were each held for 5 years.

Sept. 17 - A 10-month series of terrorist bomb attacks in France begins. One bomb in Paris kills five and injures 52.

1987

A car bomb exploded outside the back gate of the U.S. Embassy in Rome and rockets were fired at the compound from across the street. One passerby was injured in the attacks.

1988

Feb. 5 - US Marine Corps Lt. Colonel Higgins, Chief of the U.N. Truce Force kidnapped and murdered by Hezbollah.

March 16 - 4000+ Kurdish civilian bodies found after Saddam Hussein ordered nerve gas attack (weapon of mass destruction) in northern Iraq, after they revolted against his rule from Baghdad. 1.5 million Relocated, 200,000 disappeared.

April 5 - 122 held hostage after a Kuwaiti Boeing 747 was hijacked and diverted to Iran, then Cyprus. Kuwait refused requests by hijackers to release 17 convicted terrorists. After 15 days, the hijackers were granted asylum in Algeria and released their hostages.

June 26 - US Naval Attaché murdered in Athens, Greece.

Dec. 21 - Pan Am Flight 103 - Boeing 747 from London to New York, blown up over Lockerbie, Scotland, by a bomb. All 259 passengers and 11 on the ground were murdered, including 35 Syracuse University students and many U.S. military personnel.

1989

June 12 - A bomb exploded aboard an unoccupied boat used by U.S. consular staff.

Sept. 19 - 171 passengers murdered when French UTA flight 772 explodes in mid-air over Niger.

October 11 - Izmir, Turkey. A bomb went off outside a U.S. military PX.

1990

Feb. - Attack of tour bus in Egypt murdering 11 people.

1991

Feb. 7 - Incirlik Air Base, Turkey, U.S. civilian contractor shot as he was getting into his car.

Oct. 28 - Ankara, Turkey. Victor Marwick, an American soldier serving at the Turkish-American base, Tus log, was murdered and his wife wounded in a car bomb attack.

Oct. 28 - Two car bombings murdering a U.S. Air Force Sergeant and severely wounded an Egyptian diplomat in Istanbul.

Nov. 8 - Bomb destroyed part of the American University in Beirut, murdering one and wounding 12.

1992

March 17 - Israeli Embassy in Buenos Aires, Argentina, destroyed by bomb murdering 29, and injuring 60.

Hotel in Yemen bombed and U.S. service members murdered, Operation Restore Hope.

1993

Jan. 25, Virginia, U.S.A. A Pakistani terrorist opened fire with AK-47 on CIA employees standing outside the building. Two agents, Frank Darling and Bennett Lansing, were murdered and three others wounded.

Feb. 26 - World Trade Center in New York badly damaged by a massive bomb by Islamic terrorists. The van bomb was planted in an underground garage, left six people dead and 1042 injured and almost 2 billion dollars in damage.

Feb. 26 - A bomb exploded inside a cafe in downtown Cairo murdering three, and 18 wounded, two were U.S. citizens.

July 5 - In eight separate incidents, 19 Western tourists traveling in southeastern Turkey, were kidnapped, including U.S. citizen Starger, after weeks in captivity, they were released.

Oct - Murdered of U. S. soldiers in Somalia.

1994

July 18 - 86 civilians murdered and 300 wounded in bomb attack on Jewish social center in Buenos Aires, Argentina.

July 26 - Israeli Embassy in London is car-bombed, wounding 20.

Air France Flight 8969 is hijacked to crash the plane in Paris but didn't succeed.
A small bomb explodes on board Philippine Airlines flight 434, murdering a Japanese businessman.

1995

Jan. 22 - Islamic Jihad militants blow themselves up amid a group of soldiers near Netanya, murdering 21. Operation Bojinka is discovered on a laptop in a Manila, Philippines apartment, in which Osama bin Laden was planning to blow up 12 planes as they flew to the U.S., and kill the Pope.

March 8 - Attack on US Diplomats in Pakistan.

April 9 - Islamic Jihad suicide bomber attacks military convoy in Gaza, murdering seven soldiers and an American tourist.

May 5 - Five foreign oil workers murdered by Islamic GIA terrorists in Algeria.

June 26 - Assassination attempt made against Egyptian President Honsi Mubarak by Islamic radicals who ambushed his motorcade.

July 4 - Six tourists, including two U.S. citizens were taken hostage in Kashmir, India. Terrorists demanded the release of Muslim militants held in Indian prisons. On Aug. 13, the decapitated body of the Norwegian hostage was found with a note stating that the other hostages also would be murdered if the group's demands were not met. They were not and all other hostages were murdered in 1996 by the terrorists.

July 25 - Islamic terrorists explode bomb in metro station in Paris, France, murdered 7 people and injuring 84.

Nov. 13 - Car bomb exploded at US Army Office of the Program Manager for Saudi Arabian National Guard Modernization, in Saudi Arabia, murdered seven, five of them U.S. citizens, and wounding nearly a hundred.

Nov. 19 - Islamic radicals' plant bomb in Egyptian embassy in Pakistan murdering 17.

Dec. 11 - 15 concurrent car bombings in Algiers kills 15 civilians and over 200 injured.

1996

Feb. 11 - Terrorists explode car bomb in Algiers murdered 17. The following month, 2 more murdered in another bomb and 10 are murdered in a train ambush in western Algeria.

Feb. 25 - A suicide bomber blew up a commuter bus in Jerusalem, murdered 26, including three U.S. citizens, and injuring 80 others, among them another two U.S. citizens.

April 19 - Eighteen Greek tourists were gunned down near the historic Pyramids in Egypt by Islamic terrorists aiming to destroy the country's tourist industry.

May - Osama bin Laden unites the Islamic Fundamentalists worldwide in their Jihad against Jews and Western Gentiles, such as al-Qaeda, Palestinian Authority, Hezbollah, Hamas, Mujahedeen, using the Taliban's organization to help fund the operations.

June 25 - Terrorists explode a truck bomb next to a USAF Khobar Towers housing facility at Dhahran, Saudi Arabia, murdered 19 American service members and 515 injured including 240 U.S. personnel.

Islamic terrorists attack tourists in Luxor, Egypt, murdered 71 people, most of them vacationers.

Aug. 26 - Sudan Airways A310 Airbus airliner hijacked on route to Jordan and diverted to England. British authorities negotiate with hijackers who release all the 13 crew and 180 passengers unharmed.

Dec. 3 - A bomb exploded aboard a Paris subway train, murdering four and injuring 86 persons, including a U.S. citizen.

A terrorist opened fire on tourists at an observation deck atop the Empire State Building in New York City, murdered a Danish national and wounding visitors from the US, Argentina, Switzerland and France before turning the gun on himself.

Dec. 23 - A car bomb in the Algerian capital, Algiers, kills three and injures 70 people in cafe near the port. Again, a week later, a car bomb kills 28 people and injures 35 people. Third car bomb in the past two weeks, murdered an additional 13 people and injuring more than 250.

1997

Jan. 2 - Major cities worldwide and U.S. get letter bombs with Egyptian postmarks at newspaper bureaus in DC, New York, London, Riyadh, S.A., and Leavenworth, KN. Experts defused all but the 1 in London, injuring two people.

Jan. 7 to 21st - Islamic terrorist rampage during these 14 days with car bombs and beheadings in Algiers, 238 dead, and 139 wounded.

Feb. 23 - Palestinian gunman opened fire on tourists at an observation deck atop the Empire State building in New York, murdered 1 and wounding over a dozen visitors before turning the gun on himself.

March 7 - Two murdered in bus bomb attack in Beijing, China.

April - Terrorists behead innocent civilians this whole month with a total of 272 murdered and over 100 injured. Knives, axes and chainsaws were used and many of the bodies were burned while still alive.

Sept. 18, 9 German tourists murdered when Muslims firebombed bus in Cairo, Egypt.

Nov. 12, 2 Terrorists shot to death four U.S. auditors of a Texas petroleum company and their driver at a Sheraton Hotel in Karachi, Pakistan.

Nov. 17, 58 western tourists murdered and 30 injured in gun attack at historic monuments in southern Egypt. Six of the Islamic terrorists are thankfully killed in shootout with police.

1998

Jan. 15 - U.S. Embassy bombing in Peru.

Feb. 23 (Published) - A Statement signed by many Islamic Jihad Leaders from most Muslim countries, first by Sheikh Osama Bin-Laden: "In compliance with God's order, we issue the following fatwa to all Muslims: The ruling to kill the Americans and their allies–civilians and military–is an individual duty for every Muslim who can, in any country in which it is possible... We — with Allah's help — call on every Muslim who believes in God and wishes to be rewarded, to comply with Allah's order to kill the Americans and plunder their money wherever and whenever they find it. Unless you go forth, Allah will punish you with a grievous penalty, and put others in your place." Religion of peace, say it again asshole Presidents of the US.

Aug. 7 - Simultaneous bombs in US Embassies in Kenya, and Tanzania, heavily damaged by massive attacks. In the Nairobi attack 292 people were murdered, including 12 Americans and 5,000 injured. 10 people were murdered and 86 injured in Tanzania incident for a total, of 302 dead, 5086 injured within an hour.

Aug. 25 - three people murdered and 25 injured in bomb attack on Planet Hollywood restaurant in Cape Town, South Africa.

Dec. 28 - 16 Western tourists kidnapped 12 Britons, 2 U.S. citizens, and 2 Australians on the main road to Aden, Yemen. Four victims were murdered during a rescue attempt the next day.

1999

Aug. 31 to Sept. 22nd - Russian apartment bombings kill almost 300 and injured 100.

Oct. 31 - Egypt Air Flight 990 crashed off the U.S. coast of Massachusetts, murdering all 217 people on board, including 100 Americans.

Nov. 12 - Six rockets were fired at the U.S. and U.N. offices in Islamabad, Pakistan.

Dec. - Millennium terror plots foiled as customs agents arrest a man smuggling in explosives. Plan to attack Los Angeles airport and other sites intercepted by CIA. In addition, Jordanian authorities foil a plot to bomb US tourists in Jordan, pick up 28 suspects.

Indian Airlines Flight 814, on route to Delhi, India is hijacked, 1 passenger is murdered. After negotiations with the Taliban, the hostages are released.

2000

The last of the 2000 millennium attack plots fails, as the boat meant to bomb the USS Sullivan's sinks.

Oct. 12 - A suicide boat exploded next to the U.S.S. Cole (guided-missile destroyer), blowing a hole 40 feet in diameter, murdering 17 American sailors and injuring 39.

2001

Feb. 5 - A bomb blast in Moscow's Byelorusskaya subway station injures 15 people.

March 28 - Bombing at bus stop in Yemen. U.S. citizens injured including a 15-year-old boy from NY.

Aug. 9 - Bombing at Sbarro's pizzeria, murdered 15 and wounded over 90, 2 of which were U.S. citizens.

Sept. 9-23 England, Cambridge 1 murdered. A 17-year-old was beaten with a hammer and stabbed to death by Muslim gang in Britain. (Ross Parker murder).

September 11 2001, nineteen Al-Qaida terrorists hijacked four American passenger planes in a coordinated attack on U.S. soil. Nearly two hundred Americans were murdered by the terrorists who hijacked American Airlines flight 77 and flew it into the pentagon, collapsing its western side. Meanwhile, two other planes, American Airlines flight 11th and United Airlines flight 175 were flown into the north and south towers of the world trade center in New York City. Both 110-story towers collapsed murdering 2752 people. A fourth plane, United Airlines flight 93 was flown by a terrorist diverting the flight to Washington, D.C. however, passengers fought the hijackers, and the plane crashed in a field near Shanksville, Pennsylvania murdering 40 passengers.

This horrible event I foretold in my NAVSSES and NAVSEA books would happen, if Washington government system did not move away from the coast. Farther inland would have given the military and our representative's time to react. It could have ended worse. This was simply a repeat of Pearl Harbor and what can happen under political correctness. I say it again, stop the madrassas teachings mentality that is an ongoing problem in the Muslim world, funded by the Saudi.

2002

February 16, Muslims snipers Lee Boyd Malvo and John Allen Muhammad kill Keenya A Cook in Tacoma, Washington. The snipers would kill 21 more people in a crime wave that stretch from coast to coast. September 23 snipers murdered Jerry Ray Taylor, 60, James D. Martin, 55, Paul J. Laruffa, 55, Million A. Woldemaian, 41, Claudine Lee Parker, 52, Kellie Adams, 24, Hong M. Ballenger, 45, James D. Martin, 55, James L. Sonny Buchhanan, 39, Premkumar A. Walekar, 54, Sarah Ramos, 34, Lori Lewis Rivera, 25, and Pascal Charlot, 72. Wounded are Caroline Seawell, 43, Muhammad Rashid, 32, Rupinder Benny Obero, 22, Iran Brown, 13, and Paul J. Laruffa, 55. Others...

June 2 England, Orrington, 1 murdered. 33-year-old, British man beaten to death by a Muslim gang.

Oct. 26 Russia, Moscow 129 murdered and 150 injured. Chechen Muslims storm a theater and hold 916 people hostage in appalling conditions. Several are shot and murdered and others die in the rescue attempt.

New York, BROOKLYN BRIDGE – In 2002, Iyman Faris, a U.S.-based Al-Qaeda operative, planned to cut the Brooklyn Bridge's support cables at the direction of 9/11 mastermind Khalid Sheikh Mohammed. However, as a testament to NYPD terrorism deterrence efforts, Faris called off the plot, indicating to al-Qaeda leaders "the weather is too hot." NYPD's 24-hour coverage of the bridge, much of which was put in place following 9/11 and intentionally made highly visible, played a large role in Faris' decision to abandon the plot. Faris was arrested in 2003, pleaded guilty, and sentenced to 20 years in federal prison for providing material support and resources to al-Qaeda, among other charges. Knowing that the city's bridges and critical infrastructure remain attractive terrorist targets, the NYPD maintains heightened security around such facilities.

2003

Jan. 11, England. Birmingham 1 murdered. 21-year-old woman stabbed to death by Pakistani on her wedding day for rejecting an arranged Muslim marriage.

Jan. 14 England, Manchester 1 murdered and 3 injured. A police detective and father of three is stabbed to death by a Muslim terrorist.

July 5 Russia Moscow 14 murdered and 24 injured. Two Fedayeen suicide bombers, both female, kill fourteen young people and injure at least two dozen others attending a rock concert.

July 10 Russia, Moscow 1 murdered. Security officer attempting to defuse a female Fedayeen bomb is murdered.

Aug. 1 Russia, Mozdok 50 murdered and 100 injured. Muslim suicide bomber drives into a hospital and kills at least fifty. More than one hundred are injured in the blast.

Aug. 25 Russia, Kasnodar 3 murdered and 17 injured. Three people were murdered in a series of bombings at a cafe and bus stop by Muslim terrorists.

Sept. 3 Russia. Kislovodsk 5 murdered and 29 injured. Mujahideen terrorist bombing of a commuter train leaves five civilians dead and about thirty injured.

Sept. 11 England, Bradford 1 murdered. A 17-year-old girl is strangled by her family for resisting an arranged marriage.

Sept. 15 Russia, Magas 3 murdered and 25 injured. Fedayeen truck bombing kills at least three people and injures more than twenty-five others.

Nov. 19 France, Paris 2 murdered. Two Jews are brutally murdered by Muslims in separate attacks in Paris. One has his throat slit and eyes gouged while a 53-year old mother is stabbed 27 times in the neck and chest.

Dec. 5 Russia, Yessentuki 44 murdered and 150 injured. Mujahedeen suicide bomber detonates explosive on a Russian commuter train carrying civilians to work. At forty-four people, including children eventually die and about one-hundred and fifty others are injured.

Dec. 9 Russia, Moscow 6 murdered and 14 injured. Female Fedayeen suicide bomber kills six people near the Kremlin and injures at least fourteen, including several college students.

SUBWAY CYANIDE ATTACK – In 2003, al-Qaeda had planned to release cyanide gas in New York City's subway system, which carries more than 5,000,000 passengers on an average weekday, as well as targeted other public places for attack. According to a U.S. government official familiar with the plot, the plan was called off by Osama bin Laden's second in command, Ayman al-Zawahiri, for unclear reasons. The NYPD took appropriate precautions after becoming aware of the plot.

2004

Feb. 3 Russia, Vladikavkaz 2 murdered and 10 injured. Two people, including a woman are murdered, and at least ten others injured by a car bomb near the Chechen border.

Feb. 6 Russia, Moscow 40 murdered and 134 injured. Forty people are murdered by a female Fedayeen suicide bomber as they were commuting to work on a Moscow subway. About one-hundred and thirty-four are injured.

Mar. 11 Spain, Madrid 201 murdered and 1841 injured. Ten coordinated al-Qaeda bomb blasts on commuter trains during the rush hour leave over two-hundred people dead and some fifteen hundred injured.

Mar. 14 Scotland, Glasgow 1 murdered. Five Pakistani immigrants abduct, torture and then burn alive a 15-year-old Scottish teen in a horrendous attack. Three later flee the country.

Mar 16 Russia, Arkhangelsk 58 murdered and 12 injured. Fifty-eight innocent people, including nine children are murdered when Chechen terrorists remove the gas caps and cause an explosion in an apartment building.

Apr. 3 Spain, Madrid 1 murdered and 11 injured. Seven terrorists responsible for the deaths of more than two-hundred train commuters, recite the Qur'an and then blow themselves up. One police officer is murdered.

Jun 4 Russia, Samara 10 murdered and 39 injured. Ten people are murdered in a bomb explosion in an outdoor market. Another forty are injured by the blast, which is attributed to militant Muslims.

Jun. 9 England, Brixton 1 murdered. A 21-year-old man is stabbed to death by Muslim gang members for refusing to convert to Islam.

July 9 Russia, Moscow I murdered. An American journalist of Forbes magazine is assassinated by Islamic separatists.

July 19 Russia, Voronezh 2 murdered and 5 injured. Islamic terrorists blow up a bus stop, murdered two civilians and injuring five more.

Herald Square Shahawar Matin Siraj and James Elshafay plotted in 2004 to place explosive devices in the Herald Square Subway Station in Manhattan. Elshafay had already considered potential targets by the time he met an NYPD informant in early 2004. In recorded conversation, Siraje expressed desire to bomb bridges and subway stations, and cited misdeeds by American forces in Iraq as eight motivating factor. Siraj and Elshafay conducted surveillance of Harald Squirt Station late August 2004 and drew a crude diagram to aid in placing the explosives; they were arrested a few days later.

Elshafay pleaded guilty to conspiracy to damaged or destroyed a subway station by means of an explosive. Siraj was found guilty in 2006 of conspiracy to place and detonate an explosives in a public transportation system, conspiracy to damage and destroy by means of an explosive a building or vehicle, conspiracy to wreck and disable a mass transportation vehicle; and conspiracy to place destructive device in or near a facility used in the operation of a mass transportation. He was subsequently sentenced to 30 years in prison shepherding the case from the initial lead to Federal prosecution required close cooperation with the U.S. Attorney's office for the Eastern District of New York

Aug. 5 England, West Bromwich 1 murdered. Shopkeeper is brutally beaten to death by members of a Muslim family upset over the presumed "taboo" relationship between his son and their Pakistani daughter.

Aug. 24 Russia, Moscow 89 murdered. Militant Muslims hijack two Russian passenger airliners, and then murder all eighty-nine people, including women and children on board the two planes. The terrorist group Islambouli Brigade claims responsibility

Aug. 31 Russia, Moscow 11 murdered and 51 injured. A female suicide bomber kills eleven rush-hour commuters at a subway station in Moscow. Fifty-one others are injured.

Sept. 1 Russia, Beslan 16 murdered and 14 injured. At least sixteen people are murdered as Mujahedeen terrorists invade a school, taking more than a hundred children hostage. Children are made to stand in windows with suicide bombers behind them.

Sept. 3 Russia, Beslan 344 murdered and 600 injured. Islamic militants shoot fleeing children in the back, and then blow them up, along with their mothers and teachers with nail-packed bombs. Others are crushed or burned to death from the effects of the bombs. More than three-hundred innocents slaughtered.

Oct. 8 France, Paris 10 injured. An Islamic extremist group plants a bomb outside the Indonesian embassy in Paris, injuring ten.

Nov. 2 Netherlands, Amsterdam 1 murdered and 1 injured. Dutch filmmaker (Grandnephew of painter Van Gogh) shot to death by a 26-year-old Moroccan after making a film critical of Islam.

Nov. 9 Russia, Aul Kumysh 7 murdered. Local Islamists are tied to the burned bodies of seven missing persons.

Nov. 9 Russia, Moscow 2 murdered and 1 injured. Islamic terrorists set off a car bomb on a city street, murdering two civilians.

Nov. 13 England, London 1 murdered. A 30-year-old computer worker is brutally assaulted and slain by three Pakistanis.

Nov. 18 Belgium, Antwerp 1 murdered. Synagogue worker gunned down on the streets of Antwerp.

Nov. 20 England, Oxford 1 murdered. A Bangladeshi man and his two sons stab a 19-year-old to death in his car in an honor murdered after an affair with their daughter.

2005

Feb. 7 Germany, Berlin 1 murdered. A 23-year-old woman is murdered by her youngest brother at a bus stop because she 'dishonored' the family by refusing to marry her cousin.

Apr. 23 England, Southall 1 murdered. A woman is brutally stabbed to death by her brother and cousin after refusing an arranged marriage.

Jun. 12 Russia, Uzunova 15 injured. Fifteen people are injured when a bomb believed to be planted by Chechen terrorists derails a commuter train

Jun 17 Russia, Astrakhan 2 murdered and 1 injured. Islamic gunmen are thought responsible for an attack on a hospital, in which two patients were shot to death in their beds.

July 7 England, London 52 murdered and 750 injured. Islamic terrorists massacre more than fifty commuters on three separate subway trains and a double-decker bus on the street with four suicide bombs. Over seven-hundred people are injured.

Sept. 23 Denmark, Slagelse 1 murdered and 1 injured. Pakistani man guns down his 19-year-old sister and injures her husband in a public honor murdered in Denmark.

Oct. 23 England, Birmingham 1 murdered and 1 injured. Pakistanis stab a 24-year-old Christian man senselessly to death in what is either a racial or religious attack.

Nov. 7 France, Paris 1 murdered. A 61-year-old retiree is beaten to death by Muslim youth for trying to extinguish a fire that they started.

Nov. 18 Sweden, Hogsby 1 murdered. 20-year-old man is beaten with an iron bar, doused with oil and stabbed 23 times by the family of his lover in an honor murdered.

2006

JFK Airport beginning in 2006, four men plotted to detonate the jet-fuel storage tanks and supply lines for John F. Kennedy Airport, in order to cause wide scale destruction and economic disruption in an attack they intended to dwarf 9/11. Through the joint terrorism task force, the NYPD worked with the FBI, which placed an informant next to the principal plotter, Russel Defreit was, a native of Guyans and Brocklyn resident who was an Airport cargo handler. Defreitas's accomplices were Abdul Kadir, former parliament Arian from Guyana with admitted ties to Iran; Abel Nur of Guyana; and Kareen Ibrahim of Trinidad and Tobago. Relying in part on Defreitas' knowledge, the men conducted extensive surveillance of the Airport and traveled to Guyana and Trinidad and Tobago to attempt to secure the support of Jamaat Al-Muslimeen, an Islamic extremist group operating in the region. The group also discussed contacting Adnan Shukrijumah, an Al-Qaida explosive expert believed to be in the Caribbean at the time. Kadir was sentenced to life in prison and 2010; Nur was sentenced to 15 years in 2011 after pleading guilty to maternal support the previous year; Ibrahim received life in 2012. All three were extradited to the United States to stand trial. Defeit was arrested in New York and received a life sentence in 2011 after being convicted of conspiracy to attack a public transportation system, conspiracy to destroy a building by fire or explosives, conspiracy to attack aircraft and aircraft material; conspiracy to destroy international Airport facilities; and conspiracy to attack in mass transportation facility.

Jan. 4 Russia, Gimry 1 murdered and 8 injured. One Russian is murdered by Chechen Mujahideen who infiltrated the border.

Feb. 2 Russia, Vladikavkaz 2 murdered and 16 injured. Muslim separatists are suspected to be behind three bombings at gambling establishments that kill a young man and woman.

Feb. 13 France, Saint Genevieve des Bois 1 murdered. A young Jewish man is kidnapped by a Muslim gang and tortured for three weeks before expiring of his wounds.

A New York stock exchange and Citigroup headquarters Durin Barot (AKA -ISSA) was sentenced to life in prison by a United Kingdom court in 2006 after pleading guilty to a planning to attack several targets both in the UK and the U.S. Including the New York Stock Exchange Citigroup headquarters in midtown Manhattan and the Prudential building in Newark, NJ. In addition, Barot filmed reconnaissance during a trip to United States and March 2001 that included shots of the world trade center. He also targeted the Office of the International Monetary Fund, and the World Bank in Washington, DC, and hotels and railway stations in London. Barot was arrested by British police in August 2004, shortly after U.S. authorities raised the terror alert level based on intelligence that Al-Qaeda had conducted an extensive reconnaissance of financial institutions in the U.S. to discuss security, deploying tactical teams to high-threat locations, and increasing vehicle inspections. Seven of Barot accomplices were given long prison sentences by British Court in 2007 for their involvement in the plot.

Mar. 10 England, Birmingham 1 murdered. A 6-year-old is burned to death when two Muslims burn down her family's house in an attempted honor murdered.

May 21 England, Leeds 1 murdered. A 19-year-old woman is beaten to death by her family, who claim that she had an 'evil spirit.'

Path train and World Trade Center retaining wall. July 2006, the FBI revealed it had uncovered a plot involving an attack on a path commuter train tunnel connecting New York and New Jersey, the placement of suicide bombers on trains, and the destruction of the retaining wall separating the Hudson River from the World Trade Center in the hopes of causing massive flooding in the city's financial district. The plot was uncovered in its early stages to a yearlong FBI investigation that included the monitoring of Internet chat rooms frequented by extremists, and involved at least eight suspects spread over several countries. The plot alleged mastermind Al-Qaeda affiliated Assem Hammoud of Lebanon, was taken into custody by authorities there. Hammoud said he was acting on orders of Osama Bin Laden and that he was planning to travel to Pakistan to receive training at Al-Qaeda camp. Another suspect was arrested in Canada and a third in England.

Transatlantic plot in a series of three trials spanning 2008 to 2010, eight men were convicted in Britain, of attempting two simultaneous detonate explosives in seven airline airliners traveling from London to several North American metropolises, including New York, British authorities also sought Rashid Rauf, a 27 year-old Briton of Pakistan descent and a prominent Al Qaida operative, as a main suspect in the plot. After Rauf's arrest in Pakistan in August 2006, his detention led to the arrest of 25 additional suspects in Britain. Authorities believed the plan involved the use of peroxide based liquid explosives that could evade air-travel security measures in place at the time. The discovery of a plot involved cooperation between American and British authorities

June 17, Muslim gunmen Mujtaba Rabbani Jabbar, 24, shot Schrum three times in the upper body, walked into the lobby, placed his gun on a counter and waited for police.

June 25 2006 Michael Julius Ford, a 22-year-old convert to Islam, uses a long barrel handgun to shoot four coworkers and a police officer at a Denver, Colorado, Safeway, claiming the attack was Allah's choice. One person died in the shooting spree. When Ford fired at police, he was shot and murdered.

July 28, 2006 Muslim from Pakistan Man Naveed Afzal Haq shot six women, murdered one, at the Jewish federation of greater Seattle building in Seattle, Washington. Haq grabbed a 14-year-old girl and used her as a hostage during the attack. Officials classified the attack as a hate crime rather than terrorism.

Aug. 7 Russia, Karachaevsk 1 murdered. A local Imam is gunned down by Islamists for performing healing.

Aug. 12 Italy, Brescia 1 murdered. A 20-year-old girl is murdered by her family for having a relationship with a non-Muslim.

Sept. 25 Russia, Kislovodsk 1 murdered. The Jamaat terrorist group claims responsibility for the Ramadan shooting of an imam.

Nov. 1 England, Blackburn 5 murdered. A conservative Muslim man burns his family to death in a fire over concerns that they were becoming too westernized.

NY, Brooklin. 2006, Uzair Paracha, a Brooklyn resident, was sentenced to 30 years in federal prison after he was convicted of attempting to help al-Qaeda operative Majid Khan enter the United States, to attack gas tanks in a plot developed alongside 9/11 planner Khalid Sheikh Mohammed. In early 2003, Paracha impersonated Khan in dealings with the Immigration and Naturalization Service (INS), and agreed to use Khan's credit card to make it appear Khan was in the United States rather than in Pakistan. He was also in possession of several identification documents in Khan's name, and had written instructions from Khan on how to pose as Khan in dealing with the INS. Paracha was found guilty in 2005 on charges including conspiracy to provide and providing material support to al-Qaeda; conspiracy to provide, and providing funds, goods, or services to al-Qaeda; and identification document fraud committed to facilitate an act of international terrorism. Majid Khan pleaded guilty in February 2012 in a military court at Guantanamo to charges stemming from his involvement with al-Qaeda and admitted to the gas tank plot, planning to assassinate Pakistan's President Musharraf, and complicity in a 2003 bombing of a Marriot hotel in Jakarta, Indonesia. The NYPD cooperated with federal authorities through the Joint Terrorism Task Force to uncover Paracha's plan.

Uzair Paracha's father, Saifullah Paracha, also was alleged to have aided al-Qaeda. The senior Paracha worked with Khalid Sheikh Mohammad to devise a way to smuggle explosives – including possibly nuclear weapons – into the United States using the New

York office of Paracha's import-export business. Saifullah Paracha, who attended the New York Institute of Technology and worked in the city for over a decade, was arrested in 2003 after Uzair stated to authorities that his father was a militant.

2007

Jun. 30 Scotland, Glasgow 5 injured. Hoping for mass casualties, Islamic radicals ram a car filled with gas canisters into the main entrance of an airport.

July 4 England, Sheffield 1 murdered. A Muslim gang beats a man to death for adultery.

July 6 England, Stoke 1 murdered. A father of seven is stabbed to death by his Muslim neighbors, apparently over his anti-immigration views.

July 18 Russia. Kizilyurt 4 murdered and 3 injured. Islamic separatists are suspected in the bombing of a school playground that kills four policemen.

Aug. 13 Russia, Novgorod 60 injured. A militant Islamic group derails a commuter train with a bomb, injuring sixty people.

Oct. 10 Austria, Wimpassing 1 klled. In an 'honor attack', a Muslim shoots a man, and then cuts off his penis.

Oct. 23 England, Leeds 1 murdered. A 19-year-old Catholic girl is stabbed to death by a Muslim who said she was too 'sexually provocative.'

Oct. 24 Macedonia, Tanusevci 1 murdered and 2 injured. Muslim terrorists kill a police officer and injure two others in a shooting attack.

Oct. 27 Belgium, Mons 1 murdered. A Pakistani family murders their daughter for moving in with a non-Muslim Belgian.

Oct. 31 Russia, Togliatti 8 murdered and 50 injured. A bomb set on the floor of a commuter bus by suspected Islamic militants kills eight.

Nov. 4 Russia, Kabardino-Bal 9 murdered. Islamic militants capture, bind, and shoot nine civilian hunters to death in a heavily wooded area.

Nov. 19 Russia, Nalchik 1 murdered and 2 injured. A Russian policeman is murdered in a shooting attack by Mujahideen.

Nov. 22 Russia, Bratsk 5 murdered and 13 injured. A young girl is among five people are murdered when Islamic radicals bomb a passenger bus.

Dec. 5 Russia, Stary Cherek 1 murdered. A police officer is gunned down by Muslim militants.

Dec. 9 Russia, Nevinnomysk 2 murdered and 4 injured. Islamic terrorists bomb a passenger bus, murdered two Russians.

2008

January 1, 2008 Egyptian born cab driver Yasir Said shoots and kills his two daughters in Irving, Texas, because they were dating non-Muslim boys. The daughters had run away from home a week earlier, fearing their father would kill them.

Feb. 3 Sweden, Malmo 1 murdered. A 16-year-old girl dies after being pushed from the balcony in a suspected honor murdered by her brother.

Feb. 28 Germany, Odenwald 3 murdered. Muslims ask three innocent Christians to identify their religion, then brutally execute them.

Mar. 10 England, Liverpool 1 murdered. A 17-year-old is beaten to death by other Muslims who accused him of violating Islamic law by drinking alcohol.

May 15 Germany, Hamburg 1 murdered. A 16-year-old girl is stabbed to death by her brother in an honor murdered prompted by her 'Western lifestyle.'

June 12 England, Forest Gate 1 injured. A Hindu man is set on fire for dating a Muslim girl.

June 20 France, Paris 1 injured. A 17-year-old Hassidic Jew is beaten into a coma by Muslim immigrants.

July 6, 2008 Muslim Pakistan Manchaudry Rashid, 56, strangled his 25-year-old daughter in Jonesboro, Georgia, after she said she wanted out of an arranged marriage. Police said the daughter, Sandela Kanwal, had argued with her father about the arrangement of her marriage to a man in Chicago. An officer explained, at some point during the altercation, he ended up murdered his daughter.

Aug. 12 Germany, Ruesselsheim 1 murdered. A 55-year-old woman is shot to death in an honor attack involving two Muslim groups.

Sept. 14 Russia, Karachayevo-Cherk. 1 murdered and 2 injured. A local cop is gunned down outside his home by Muslim terrorists.

Nov. 6 Russia, Vladikavkaz 11 murdered and 40 injured. A female suicide bomber strikes at a marketplace bus stop, murdering at least eleven passengers.

Nov. 19 England, Woolwich 1 murdered. A failed asylum seeker from Algeria beats a gay man to death who took him in.

Nov. 26 Russia, Vladikavkaz 1 murdered. A mayor is assassinated by local terrorists, who call him an "enemy of Allah."

Dec. 14 England, West Yorkshire 1 injured. A Muslim youth brutally stabs a 51-year-old at random after telling him that he is walking through an area of Britain that 'Muslims rule.'

Dec. 31 Denmark, Odense 2 injured. A Muslim shoots two Jewish vendors at a shopping mall.

2009

February 12, 2009 Pakistani American Muzzammil Syed Hassan was the CEO of the first American Muslim TV Network broadcast in English, Bridged TV. Hassan beheaded his estranged wife,Aasiya Zubair, after she filed for divorce. Her body was found at the TV station. When he was arrested, he said he felt an incredible amount of relief after he murdered the woman.

Mar. 2 Germany, Rees 1 murdered. A 20-year-old girl is clubbed to death by her brother for having sex.

Mar. 8 Russia, St. Petersburg 1 murdered. A Muslim man has his 21-year-old woman shot to death for wearing miniskirts.

Mar. 15 England, London 1 injured. A Christian minister critical of Islam is brutally beaten by local Muslims.

April 12 2009 upon learning that, they had patronized a strip club; a Muslim man shoots and kills his brother in law and another man in phoenix, Arizona.

Apr. 30 England, Manchester 1 murdered. A Sikh dies from injuries suffered when a Muslim gang severely beats him in what police call an unprovoked 'racist' attack.

May 2009, Bronx synagogues, four men placed what they believed were functioning bombs outside of Jewish targets, in the Bronx neighborhood of Riverdale and additionally constructed plans to fire missiles at military transport planes at Stewart International Airport near Newburgh, New York. Suspect, James Cromitie confided his desire to commit acts against the United States to Federal informant in 2008 and aspired to travel to Afghanistan to become a martyr, and to join Pakistani extremist groups Jaish-E- Mohammad, Cromitie recruited Ont A. Williams IV, and :Aguerre Payen to join him in the the Riverdale attacks. By April 2009 the four targeted the Riverdale Temple and nearby Riverdale Jewish center, and conducted surveillance at Steward Airport. A government informant supplied the group with an inert missile system and fake explosives. The group was arrested after they placed what they believe were functioning bombs outside of their Riverdale targets, convicted in 2010 and subsequently sentenced to 25 year terms.

June 1, 2009 In a drive by shooting, Abdulhakim Mujahid Muhammad converted to Islam, had traveled to Yemen and was deported to the U.S. for over staying his visa. He opened fired on U.S. soldiers standing in front of a Little Rock, Arkansas recruiting office. Muhammad murdered one private and injured another. When he was arrested, Mohammad explained that he had planned to kill as many soldiers as possible, and was given the assignment by Al Qaida in the Arab Peninsula.

Jun. 14 Belgium, Brussels 1 murdered. A 32-year-old woman is murdered by her brothers for refusing to wear the veil.

Jun. 24 Germany, Schweinfurt 1 murdered. A 15-year-old girl is stabbed to death by her father over her Western lifestyle.

Jun. 29 Belgium, Brussels 1 murdered. A woman is found dead, the victim of an honor murdered by her husband and brother-in-law for seeking a divorce.

July 2 England, London 1 injured. A 24-year-old man is blinded, suffers the loss of his tongue and 90% burns during an 'honor' attack in which he was forced to drink acid and had it thrown on him by angry Muslims.

July 9 France, Lyon 1 murdered. A 22-year-old woman is murdered by her 17-year-old "religious" brother, angry over a sexual affair.

July 20 Germany, Munich 1 murdered. A Muslim man stabs his ex-wife to death 'in the name of the Qur'an' for being in a relationship.

Aug. 19 Belgium, Jette 1 injured. A man who says he was sent by Allah to punish women who wear makeup, walks into a beauty salon and attacks an employee while quoting the Qur'an.

September 2009 New York City subway system plot was targeted for attack by three individuals, who planned to set off bombs in a subway during rush hour, shortly after the eighth anniversary of 9/11. Once Queens residents Najibullah Zazi and Zarein Ahmedzay, of Afghan dissent, and Bosnian Adis Medunjanin had self radicalized largely through listening to on line extremist material, including teachings by Anwar Al-Awlaki.

The trio plotted to travel to Afghanistan to fight alongside the Taliban against American and coalition forces, and said they were motivated by American actions against Muslim population overseas. Although in Pakistan in late August 2008, Ahmedeay and Medunjanin were turned around by Pakistani Security forces while trying to enter Afghanistan in a taxi. In looking for another approach to three canvassed mosques in Peshawar, Pakistan until they were put in contact with Al-Qaeda representatives. They then traveled from tribal areas in north Waziristan, were they received terrorist training from high ranking members who urged their return to the United States to carry out an attack it home, a request to which they acquiesced. Zazi received further explosives training from Al-Qaeda and the three returned to the U.S. separately. In January 2009, days after his return to the United States, Zazi moved to Aurora, Colorado where he began to experiment with explosives and eventually constructed the detonation charges for the bombs that were to be used by the trio in attacking the subway. He remained in contact with Ahmedzay and Medunjanin while in Colorado, and drove to New York from Aurora in early September 2009 with the explosive charges in his vehicle.

The plot was thwarted through an intelligence tip received by the FBI and with the cooperation of the NYPD, through the Joint Terrorism task force. Zazi and Ahmedzay pleaded guilty in 2010 to conspiracy to use a weapon of mass destruction, conspiracy to commit murder in a foreign country in providing material support to a foreign terrorist organization; they are awaiting sentencing. Medunjanin was convicted in 2012 of conspiring to use weapons of mass destruction, conspiring to commit murder of U.S. military personnel abroad, providing and conspiring to provide material support to Al-Qaida, receiving military training from Al-Qaida, conspiring and by attempting to commit an act of terrorism transcending national borders, and using firearms and destructive devices in relation to these offenses. He was later sentenced to life.

Sept. 15 Italy, Trieste 1 murdered and 1 injured. An 18-year-old girl dies from being stabbed in the throat by her father for falling in love with a non-Muslim

Sept. 20 Russia, Cherkessk 1 murdered. A moderate cleric is assassinated by Wahabbi extremists.

Oct. 2 Russia, Kabardino-Balkaria 1 murdered and 3 injured. Muslim gunmen kill a police officer in a drive-by.

Oct. 22 Russia, Plievo 1 murdered. Fundamentalists murder a shop owner for selling alcohol.

Long island railroad, Bryant Neal Vinas, of Long Island, New York, traveled to Pakistan with intent to die fighting against American forces in Afghanistan. He was later called to testify in the trial of Adis Medunjanin, one of Najibullah Zazi's co-conspirators in the September 2009 subway plot. In his testimony, Vinas stated he was motivated by a reading a radical Yemen-American cleric Anwar Al-Awake. He spent much of the time in Pakistan shopping for a group to join before ultimately ending up in north Waziristan in Pakistan's trouble areas in early 2008, and subsequently received over five weeks of terrorism training from Al Qaida. In summer, 2009 Vinas spoke to Al-Qaeda about targeting the Long Island railroad using a suitcase bomb that would be left in a car and set to detonate. He drew maps Long Island and showed that all LIRR trains pass through one tunnel when entering Manhattan; suggesting that an explosive in the tunnel would cause the most damage. Pakistan authorities arrested Vinas in November 2008 and he pleaded guilty in the United States to Federal charges of conspiracy to murder, Material support to Al-Qaeda and receiving military training from Al-Qaeda.

November 2009 Iraq born Muslim man Faleh Hassan Almaleki, 48 intentionally hit his draughter with his car and murdered her, because she had becoming too westernized. He also attacked the mother of the girl's boyfriend. Police said it occurred because her not following traditional family values. He felt she was becoming too westernized, and he didn't like that his daughter had backed out of an arranged marriage.

November 5, 2009 Muslim gunmen Nidal Malik Hassan, and army psychiatrist, fatally shoots/murders 13 people and wound 30 others at fort hood, Texas.

Nov. 19 Russia, Moscow 1 murdered and 1 injured. An anti-Islam priest is assassinated in his own church by a suspected Muslim gunman.

Nov.27 Russia, Bologoye 26 murdered and 96 injured. Twenty-six passengers are murdered when Islamic terrorists derail a train with a bomb.

December 4, 2009, a Muslim graduate student from Saudi Arabia, Abdulsalam Al-Zahrani, stabbed his non-Muslim Islamic studies professor, Richard G Antoun, to deaths to avenge persecuted Muslims. One of his roommate said he was all the time shouting in Arabic, shouting threats insulting his country for no reason.

2010

Jan. 12 France, Paris 1 injured. An actress-playwright is doused with petrol and nearly set on fire by three Algerians angered by her negative portrayal of Muslim men.

Feb. 3 Germany, Northrhein-Westphalia 1 murdered. A mother of four is beheaded and then has her fingers cut off in a suspected 'honor' attack by her husband.

Feb. 20 England, Huddersfield 1 murdered. A Muslim gang of five beats a Sikh shopkeeper to death with a hammer.

Mar. 29 Russia, Moscow 38 murdered and 102 injured. Female suicide bombers massacre about forty subway commuters and leave another one-hundred in agony.

April 14, 2010 a Muslim convert James A. Larry, 33, became angry that his family would not convert to Islam and shot his mother, pregnant wife, infant son and two nieces in Marquette Park, Illinois. He pleaded guilty to multiple counts of murder, attempted murder and the intentional homicide of an unborn child. He was upset that his wife and their family. He felt disrespected that they would not join his religion assistant state Attorney Jim McKay said. It didn't matter if they were young or old, pregnant or not. He wanted them dead. Larry also shot his 13-year-old nephew in the face, but the boy survived. When the man was arrested, he told officers Allah told him to kill his family, according to court records. According to a police report, he said I wish I had more bullets. I wish I had more bullets. This is the true mind set of all Muslims make no mistake. Make no mistakes Muslims can go off very easily in your mist.

Apr. 7 Russia, Baksan 2 murdered. Two police officers are gunned down in a brutal ambush by suspected Islamists.

Apr. 10 Russia, Nalchik 1 murdered. Muslim terrorists are suspected in the car bombing death of a police officer.

Apr. 23 England, Leicester 1 injured. A Sikh man is brutally beaten by a gang of Muslims, who shout "Allah" during the attack and pull off his religious necklace.

Apr. 30 France, Strasbourg 1 injured. A Jewish man is stabbed in the neck and hit in the face with an iron bar by a Muslim yelling about a Zionist conspiracy.

May 1, 2010 Times Square, Faisal Shahzad, a Pakistani American residing in Connecticut, attempted to detonate a car bomb in Times Square. Like Vinas and Zazi-Trio before him, Shahzad received terrorist training in Pakistan's Waziristan region during a trip he made to the contrary from July 2009 until February 2010. The training was provided by the Tehrik-i-Taliban Pakistan (TIP), generally refer to as the Pakistani Taliban. Upon returning to the United States, Shahzad received $12,000 in two separate payments from TIP- associated co- conspirator to aid his plot. The bomb's failure to detonate had to do in large part with the inferior components Shahzad used; Shahzad was concerned that purchasing more effective ingredients as called for by this training would alert law enforcement. Shahzad was influenced, in part, by the teachings of Anwar Al-Awlaki, and in court cited American foreign policy as a primary motive for his actions. Cooperation between NYPD and the FBI led to the identification and arrest 53 hours after the attempted bombing, as he attempted to flee the country, Shahzad pleaded guilty to all charges against him and was sentenced to life in prison.

May 1 Russia, Nalchik 1 murdered and 29 injured. Muslim radicals set off a bomb at a race track, murdered an elderly veteran of World War II.

May 10 Switzerland, Hongg 1 murdered. A 16-year-old girl is honor murdered by her father with an axe.

May 19 Russia, Dagestan 3 murdered. Muslim radicals gun down two local cops and kill a third with a bomb in neighboring Chechnya.

May 22 Russia, Prokladnyi 3 murdered. Two women and one man are gunned down in cold blood by suspected Islamic insurgents.

May 26 Russia, Starvropol 7 murdered and 40 injured. Two young girls are among seven murdered when terrorists bomb a concert hall.

Jun. 11 Russia, Nalchik 1 murdered. A cop is murdered by gunfire from a mosque.

July 12 England, London 1 injured. A religious studies teacher is badly beaten by four Muslims intent on punishing him for 'insulting Islam' by teaching girls.

July 21 Russia, Baksanskaya 2 murdered. Islamic militants murder two guards at a power plant.

Aug. 6 Russia, Baksan 2 murdered. Two security personnel are brutally shot to death while sitting in their car.

Aug. 10 Russia, Kabardino-Balkaria 2 murdered. Two people are murdered when Muslim terrorists fire at tourists at a resort.

Aug. 17 Russia, North Ossetia 2 murdered and 23 injured. Two people are dead and twenty-three others injured in a suicide attack and separate cafe bombing.

Sept. 7 Russia, Baksanenok 1 murdered. Suspected Islamists assassinate a judge.

Sept 9 Russia, Vladikavkaz 18 murdered and 123 injured. A Shahid drives an explosives-laden vehicle into a market, blasting seventeen shoppers to bits.

Sept. 29 Russia, Elbrus 2 murdered and 20 injured. A woman is among two people shot to death by Islamists.

Oct. 3 Italy, Modena 1 murdered and 1 injured. A woman is beaten to death by her own husband for trying to stop the forced marriage of her daughter, who is also put in a coma by her brother.

Oct. 8 Georgia, Gudauta 1 murdered and 2 injured. A religious leader is murdered when suspected Islamic terrorists fire into their mosque.

Oct. 9 Russia, Kabardino-Balkaria 1 murdered. A court official is murdered by suspected Muslim gunmen while walking home.

Nov. 4 Russia, Nalchik 2 murdered. Two hunters are tortured and murdered by Islamic militia.

Nov. 15 Sweden, Katrineholm 1 murdered. A 21-year-old woman is stabbed 53 times by her Muslim father, who was angered by her 'indecent' lifestyle.

Nov. 18 Russia, Oktyabrsky 2 injured. A Muslim stabs two police officers, saying he is upset that they do not allow Allah's law to be practiced.

Dec. 6 Russia, Moscow 1 murdered. An armed Muslim immigrant targets and kills a young engineer by shooting him three times in the chest and once in the head.

Dec. 11 Sweden, Stockholm 2 injured. A car bomb and suicide attack on a shopping center leaves two injured.

Dec. 12 England, Feltham 1 injured. Muslim prisoners batter a guard while yelling 'death to the Kuffar'.

Dec. 15 Russia, Nalchik 1 murdered. A moderate cleric is shot in front of his home for 'resisting religious extremism.'

Dec. 18 Russia, Kabardino- Balkaria 7 murdered and 2 injured. Seven hunters are shot to death by Islamic militants in a brutal ambush.

Dec. 23 Russia, Shalushki 2 murdered and 5 injured. Islamic militants gun down two village policemen.

2011

Jan. 11 Russia, Kenzh 1 murdered. A folk healer is murdered in his home by suspected Islamic fundamentalists.

Jan. 15 Russia, Kabardino-Balkariya 1 murdered. An Islamic militant shoots a cattle-breeder to death for refusing to finance Jihad.

Jan. 24 Russia, Moscow 37 murdered and 150 injured. Three dozen innocent people at an airport are cut to shreds by shrapnel from two suicide bombers.

Feb. 2 Russia, Chegem 5 murdered. Islamic radicals burst into a cafe and gun down five traffic cops in cold blood.

Feb. 14 Russia, Gubden 3 murdered and 26 injured. A female suicide bomber murders three people.

Feb. 19 Russia, Zayukovo 4 murdered and 1 injured. Caucasus Emirate terrorists stop a van full of ski tourists and then machine-gun them to death.

Feb. 25 Russia, Nalchik 12 injured.A dozen guards are injured when Islamists try to stage a grenade attack on a hospital.

Mar. 2 Germany, Frankfurt 2 murdered and 2 injured. A gunman yells 'Allah Akbar' and opens fire on unarmed US soldiers on a bus, murdering two.

April 30 2011, Rahim Abdul Alfetlawi, 46, shot his stepdaughter in the head at point blank range in Warren, Michigan, after she refused to adhere to strict Muslim customs. The family claimed the motive was not a religion.

Apr. 30 Bulgaria, Pazardjik 1 injured. A pastor who converted from Islam is beaten bloody in front of his church by a gang of Muslims.

Manhattan Synagogue Ahmed Ferhani, a Queens resident born in Algeria, along with Mohammad Mamdouh, a Moroccan immigrant were arrested in May 2011 in an NYPD operation in which Ferhani purchased a hand grenade, three semiautomatic pistols and ammunitions from an undercover detective. NYPD investigation into the pair revealed their desire to attack a synagogue in New York City. Ferhani was indicted under New York's anti-terrorism legislation and pleaded guilty in December 2012 to charges including conspiracy as a crime of terrorism and criminally possession of a weapon as a crime of terrorism. In his allocution, Ferhani stated that he agreed with Mamdouh to develop a plan to attack and damage a Synagogue in New York County or elsewhere in New York City, using explosives in an effort to coerce and intimidate the city's Jewish population. He further clarified that his motivation was to avenge the perceived mistreatment of Muslims Worldwide. Ferhani was sentenced in March 2013 to 10 years in state prison after his guilty plea December 2012 to terror- related charges for plotting to target New York Synagogues. The case marks the first application of New York's terror laws in it terrorism case.

May 26 Russia, Vladikavkaz 1 murdered. Muslim extremists murder a poet for offending Islam.

May. 28 Switzerland, Einsiedeln 1 murdered. A 24-year-old woman is shot to death by her strict Muslim father for leading an 'independent life'.

Jun. 26 Italy, Padua 1 murdered. A Moroccan immigrant kills his wife for becoming 'too Western'. Others support his right to 'stone the adulteress'.

Aug. 26 Norway, Jaeren 1 injured. A Christian convert from Islam is scalded with boiling water and acid at a refugee center.

September 11, 2011 three Jewish men are discovered in Waltham, Massachusetts, with their throats slit from ear to ear and nearly decapitated. Authorities believed the murderers were not random and thousands of dollars in cash and marijuana were left at the scene. According to reports, authorities believe Boston marathon bombers Tamerlan Tsarnaev and his younger brother; both Muslims may have been responsible for the triple homicide. Proof that Muslims are often taught to cut the throat of animals for training as adult when they murder non-Muslims.

Sept. 11 England, London 2 injured. Two activists are stabbed by Muslims after disparaging Islam

Returning military targeted Jose Pimentel, a native of the Dominican Republic and convert to Islam, was charged with plotting to donate bombs in and around New York City, and November 2011 used instructions on how to build a bomb published by Al-Qaida inspired magazine. After a 2 1/2 year investigation by the NYPD intelligence bureau, Pimentel was caught while assembling three bombs. Pimentel's targets included members of the armed forces who were returning from service in Iraq and Afghanistan. He also considered traveling to Temen to participate in terrorist training and claimed to have emailed radical, Yemen American cleric Anwar Al-Awlaki but received no response. However, Pimentel successfully corresponded with Jesse Morton, the founder of the website Revolution Muslim, who was sentenced in June 2012 to 11.5 years in prison for using the internet to solicit violence against individuals to include the writers of the of the popular TV satire South Park. Pimentel's criminal case is pending.

Nov. 8 Russia, Yaroslav 1 murdered. Suspected Islamists shoot a rival imam several times in the head.

Nov. 16 Russia, Moscow 1 murdered. A poet is shot five times in the head after 'angering' Islamic separatists in Chechnya

2012

January 15, 2012 A Jordanian Muslim, Ali Mahwood-Awad Irsan, 57, gunned down Iranian Medical student, Gelareh Bagherzadeh, a friend of his daughter and a Christian convert who widely denounced Islam. He later murdered his Christian son-in-law after his daughter married him without permission. Assistant Harris county district Attorney, Tammy Thomas, told a district judge, he said I. murdered that bitch and you're next. No one insults my honor as a Muslim and gets away with it.

Marcos Alonso Zea, a U.S. citizen from Brentwood, Long Island was arrested in October 2013 following a joint investigation by the FBI and the NYPD intelligence bureau. Zea was indicted on Federal terrorism charges related to his failed January 2012 attempt to travel to Yemen to join Al Qaida in the Arabian Peninsula, considered the most dangerous Al Qaida affiliate to the American interests. Zea was a friend of Kaliebe. An NYPD under cover with extensive knowledge of Yemen played a key role in determining that Zea sought to join the terrorist group. Zea is being prosecuted in the eastern district of New York.

Jan. 24 Norway, Haugesund 2 injured. Two ex-Muslim converts to Christianity are stabbed by three attackers shouting 'kuffar' (unbeliever).

Jan. 26 Russia, Kabardino-Balkaria 1 murdered. Islamists cut the throat of a Russian playing volleyball at a grammar school.

Feb. 13 Russia, Pyatigorsk 1 murdered. A cleric is taken apart by a Religion of Peace car bombing.

Feb 13 Russia, Dagestan 3 murdered and 6 injured. Three police officers are gunned down by Islamic 'separatists'

Mar. 11 France, Toulouse 1 murdered. An off-duty paratrooper is shot in the head at close range by a Muslim terrorist.

Mar. 12 Belgium, Anderlecht 1 murdered and 1 injured. A Sunni firebombs a Shiite mosque, murdered the imam.

Mar. 15 France, Montauban 2 murdered and 1 injured. Two soldiers are shot to death in an al-Qaeda drive-by attack.

Mar. 19 France, Toulouse 4 murdered. Three children under the age of seven are chased and shot in the head at a Jewish school along with their father.

Apr. 12 Macedonia, Smilkovsko 5 murdered. Five young Christian fishermen between the ages of 18 and 22 are brutally slaughtered by a group of radical Muslims at a lake.

Apr. 23 Sweden, Landskrona 1 murdered. A 19-year-old woman is stabbed to death by her younger brother for having boyfriends and wanting to live independently.

May 5 Germany, Bonn 29 injured. Twenty-nine police are injured when 'strict Muslims' attack with bottles and sticks over cartoons of Muhammad.

May 12 Germany, Bonn 2 injured. Two police officers are stabbed by an Islamist.

May 28 England, Luton 1 injured. A 19-year-old Sikh is raped in a targeted attack by an Islamic radical.

May 28 Russia, Moscow 1 injured. A journalist is slashed fifteen times with a knife outside his apartment for criticizing Islam's prophet on a radio show.

Jun. 2 France, Villeurbanne 3 injured. Three young Jewish men with skullcaps are severely beaten with hammers and iron bars by ten Muslims.

Jun. 9 Belgium, Brussels 2 injured. Two police officers are stabbed with a knife at a train station by an Islamist.

Jun 22 France, Rennes 1 murdered. A 16-year-old is violently murdered by a Muslim classmate in what is regarded as a 'racist' attack. Other Muslims have shown solidarity with the killer.

July 12 Wales, Cardiff 1 murdered. A 7-year-old boy is beaten to death by his mother for failing to memorize the Quran.

July 18 Bulgaria, Burgas 7 Murdered and 30 injured. A Shahid suicide bomber detonates on a bus carrying Israeli tourists, murdered seven and injuring dozens more.

July 19 Russia, Kazan 1 murdered and 1 injured. Two advocates of peaceful Islam are targeted by radicals. One is shot to death and the other injured in a car bomb.

Aug. 29 Georgia, Lapankuri 3 murdered. A doctor is among three people who die trying to rescue innocent hostages taken by Islamic radicals.

Aug. 29 Germany, Berlin 1 injured. A rabbi is beaten by Muslims in front of his young daughter for 'being Jewish'.

Sept. 19 France, Sarcelles 1 injured. A member of an Islamist cell throws a grenade into a kosher grocery store.

Oct. 23 Russia, North Ossetia 1 murdered and 3 injured. A Fedayeen suicide bomber takes out a local cop.

Oct. 24 Russia, Kazan 1 murdered and 1 injured. A police officer dies from injuries suffered when an Islamic militant self-detonates.

The brothers plot Raees Alam Qazi and sheheryar Alam Qazi, Pakistani brown brothers, were arrested by Federal authorities in Florida in November 2012 for charges relating to a plan to bomb popular New York City landmarks including Times Square, Wall Street and city theaters. Raees Qazi had traveled to New York allegedly to gain employment to finance the building of an explosive device and to select a target. He and his brother both were charged with conspiracy to provide material support to the terrorist and conspiring to use a weapon of mass destruction. Authorities searched Raees' Florida home and found material and instruction related to the construction of an explosive device. Raees was reportedly seeking retribution for the deaths caused by drone strikes in Afghanistan.

Dec. 5 Russia, Nalchik 1 murdered. A television journalist is murdered by suspected Muslim extremists.

Dec. 24 Germany, Bonn 1 injured. Islamic extremists slash the tongue of an Indian student who refused their offer to embrace Islam.

Dec. 25 Russia, Nalchik 1 murdered. Suspected Islamists shoot a non-Muslim twice in the head.

Dec. 26 Russia, Vladikavkaz 1 murdered. A moderate mufti is assassinated by Islamic radicals

2013

Jan. 1 Italy, Venice 1 injured. Fifteen Arab youth set upon a Jewish-American tourist with sharp objects, beating him into unconsciousness.

Jan. 28 Russia, Kabardino-Balkaria 1 murdered. An off-duty police officer is assassinated by suspected Islamic 'separatists'.

Federal reserve, Quazi Mohammad Rezwanul Ahsan Nafis,21, native of Bangladesh residing in the U.S. on a student visa, was arrested in October 2012 as he attempted to remotely detonate what he believed was a bomb in front of the Federal reserve bank of New York ,in lower Manhattan. Nafis came to law enforcement's attention in July 2012 as he unknowingly tried to recruit a confidential government source to aid in his plan to attack the United States at home. In an article Nafis had hoped would be published in

Al Qaida inspire magazine, he asserted his desire to destroy America by attacking its economy. Nafis also told the government source that he had Al Qaida contacts abroad that could assist in planning and execution of an attack. The fake explosive was assembled by Nafis and an undercover government agent. Nafis pleaded guilty in February 2013 to attempting to use a weapon of mass destruction and was subsequently sentenced to 30 years in prison. The NYPD cooperated closely with the FBI in the case through the joint terrorism task force.

February 7 2013, Yusuf Ibrahim, 28, shot two Coptic Christians to death and beheaded them in Buena Vista, New Jersey. He also removed their hands before burying their bodies in the backyard of an abandoned house. *Quran 8:12 states, when the lord was revealing to the angels, I am with you; so confirm the believers. I shall cast into the unbelievers is hearts terror, so smite above the necks, and smite every finger of them.*

Feb. 5 Denmark, Copenhagen none. A Danish cartoonist narrowly escapes an assassination attempt on his front steps from a man who fires from a yard away.

Justin Kaliebe, American Citizen Justin Kaliebe pleaded guilty in February 2013 to charges of providing material support to terrorists. The long island resident was arrested at JFK Airport in January while attempting to board a flight to Amman with the intent of reaching Yemen to join Al Qaida in the Arabian Peninsula. In conversations recorded by NYPD under over officer, Kaliebe voiced his desire to engage in violent jihad abroad and specifically to fight against the Yemen army and those who are fighting against the sharia of Allah to include United States; He made clear his willingness to die in pursuit of his goal. Kaliebe cited both Osama Bin Laden and Anwar Al-Awlaki as inspirations

Feb. 6 Russia, Nalchik 1 murdered and 1 injured. A local cop is gunned down by Islamic militants.

Feb. 18 Netherlands, Brabant 1 murdered. Islamists are suspected in the murder of a Christian convert from Iran.

Jesse Morton, Yousef Mohammad Al-Khattab, and Revolution Muslim a multi-year NYPD intelligence bureau investigation its leaders culminated in the arrest and guilty pleas of Jesse Morton and Yousef Al-Khaittabab, two New York area Muslim converts who cofounded the group. Through its efforts, the NYPD became aware of the extremist material and threats posted on the revolution Muslim revolution Muslim web page. On March 25, 2013, Shehadeh was convicted of three counts of making false statements in a matter involving international terrorism he faces up to 21 years in prison.

March 31, 2013, Reshad Reshad Riddle walked into an Ashtabula, Ohio, church and fatally shot his father after an Easter service. After the shooting, witnesses say, walked through the church holding the gun and shouting that the slaughter was the will of Allah. This is the will of god.

April 15 2013, Muslim Chechen Brothers Dzhckhar Tsarnaev and Tamerlan Tsarnaev denote two pressure cooker bombs during the Boston marathon, murdered three people and injuring an estimated 264 others. After the bombing, they murdered an MIT police officer, stole an SUV and exchanged gunfire with police. Tamerlan was shot and his brother drove over him with the stolen SUV. Tamerlan was pronounced dead at the scene. After a manhunt, police found Dzhckhar hiding in a boat in a man's backyard. Dzckhar has been sentenced to death.

Apr. 23 France, Paris 2 injured. An Iranian national attacks a Jewish father and son along a city street.

May 7 France, Roussillon 1 injured. A Muslim who had recently returned from the Haj shouts 'Allah Akbar' and stabs a police officer at random.

May 22 England, London 1 murdered. An off-duty soldier is hacked to death in the name of Allah by two Muslims.

May 25 France, Paris 1 injured. A soldier is wounded when a Muslim stabs him in the neck in a Paris shopping district.

August 4 2013, a Muslim convert, Daymond Agnew, 34, went to an Ace Hardware Store on a mission from Allah to help people before he fatally stabbed employee Daniel Joseph Stone 17 times.

Aug. 4 Germany, Brandenburg 1 murdered and 2 injured.

Oct. 12, Islamists beat an unmarried couple, causing the woman to lose her baby.

Humayoun Ghoulamnabi and Ismail Alsarabbi, in October 2013 both were arrested on state level terrorism charges for seeking to send cold weather gear and electronics to support terrorist organizations in Afghanistan and Pakistan, including the time of the pair met with a supplier to procure winter clothing including jackets and coats which were to be stored in a Jamaica, New York warehouse prior to being and sent overseas. Nabi sought the assistance of an NYPD undercover officer in delivering the gear to fighters battling western forces in Afghanistan. Nabi compared his efforts to those of Osama Bin Laden, stated his desire to build a network of supporters and sought to use a nonprofit to covertly send money overseas in furtherance of his cause.

Oct 12 Scotland, Sterling 1 murdered. A Muslim burns his 'too Westernized' wife to death after asserting that Islam teaches a man's superiority over women.

Oct. 21 Russia, Volgograd 6 murdered and 37 injured. A Muslim woman detonates an explosives-laden suicide vest on a bus, murdered six strangers

Oct. 28 England, Essex 1 murdered. A prostitute is murdered by a devout Muslim for working too close to his mosque.

Dec. 27 Russia, Pyatigorsk 3 murdered. Islamic militants detonate a car bomb that takes three lives.

Dec. 29 Russia, Volgograd 18 murdered and 51 injured. Children are among the casualties when a female suicide bomber detonates at a train station, murdered at least eighteen.

Dec. 30 Russia, Volgograd 16 murdered and 35 injured. A bus is blown up by a suicide bomber, leaving at least sixteen dead commuters.

2014

Jan 9 Russia, Stavropol Krai 6 murdered. Six victims of suspected Islamists are discovered shot in the head.

March 6, 2014, registered sex offender James Cosby, 46, is accused of bludgeoning his lesbian daughter to death and shooting her lover in Port Bolivar, Texas. Police believe he then dumped the bodies near a ferry gate. In his bedroom, Cosby had the Quran opened to a page that says homosexuality is a sin.

April 27 2014, a 30-year-old Muslim man, Ali Muhammad Brown, is accused of shooting to death two men in Seattle and a man in New Jersey. According to local reports, he told police the murdered were vengeance for U.S. actions in the Middle East. According to court documents, he said they were just kills and that he was just doing my small part as a self-styled jihadist. This is why Congress should pull the reins in on Islam. This kind of spontaneous actions by Muslims is why everyone should carry a handgun.

May 17 England, Accrington 1 injured. A political candidate is stabbed in the face by a Muslim calling him an 'infidel'

May 24 Belgium, Brussels 4 murdered. An Islamic extremist shoots four people to death outside a Jewish museum.

Jun. 17 Norway, Oslo 1 injured. A moderate imam is stabbed by a member of his mosque after denouncing radicals.

Aug. 16 Russia, Vladikavkaz 1 murdered. A moderate imam is shot seven times by suspected Islamic radicals.

September 25 2014, Alton Nolen is accused the beheading a woman in Moore, Oklahoma. Coworkers reported that Nolen had been trying to convert them to Islam. Nolen reportedly use some Arabic terms during his attack and had an interest in beheadings. Nolen told a judge, I'm Muslim. My question is, do you have any Muslims that can represent me as a Muslim? Assimilate my ASS.

Sept. 30 Georgia, Pankisi Gorge 1 injured. A woman is stabbed in the breast by her fundamentalist brother for not wearing a hijab.

Dec. 20 France, Joue-les-Tours 3 injured. A foreign-born Muslim attacks French police officer with a knife while shouting praises to Allah.

Dec. 21 France, Dijon 13 injured. A convert to Islam praises Allah as he runs down pedestrians with his car 'for the children of Palestine'.

Dec. 22 France, Nantes 1 murdered and 9 injured. One person is left clinically dead when yet another man shouting Allah Akbar plunges his car into a Christmas market.

2015

Jan. 7 France, Paris 12 murdered and 10 injured. A dozen people are slaughtered by gunmen 'avenging' the prophet at a newspaper office, which printed satirical cartoons critical of Islam.

Jan. 8 France, Montrouge 1 murdered and 1 injured. A police officer investigating a traffic accident is ambushed and murdered by a Muslim extremist. Not even is the police safe from spontaneous Muslim attacks, never mind stupid Negros shooting cops.

Jan. 9 France, Paris 4 murdered and 5 injured. Four hostages are taken and murdered by an Islamic gunman at a Jewish grocery.

Jan. 29 Ireland, North Belfast 1 murdered. An immigrant from Somalia stabs a man to death on the street while yelling a 'Jihadi war cry'

Feb. 3 France, Nice 3 injured. Three French soldiers standing guard at a Jewish center are stabbed by a radical Muslim.

Feb. 14 Denmark, Copenhagen 1 murdered and 3 injured. A gunman praises Allah and fires into a cafe hosting a free speech event organized by a cartoonist critical of Islam, murdered one participant.

Feb. 15 Denmark, Copenhagen 1 murdered and 2 injured. A 37-year-old Jewish man guarding a synagogue is gunned down by a Muslim radical.

Mar. 10 Austria, Liesing 1 murdered. A 'migrant' stabs an older man to death on the grounds that his music was against Islam.

Apr. 16 Italy, Sicily 12 murdered. A dozen Christians on a refugee boat are thrown to their deaths by Muslims.

Apr. 19 France, Villejuif 1 murdered. A 24-year-old woman is shot to death by an Islamic extremist who planned a shooting rampage.

May 3, 2015, Garland, Texas, Pamela Geller, along with her group the American Freedom Defense Initiative, posted a draw Muhammad event. Elton Simpson and Nadir Socfi of Phoenix responded to a call to avenge the prophet, and travel to Garland where they were shot and killed by a security guard after opening fire, an apparent attempt to get into the building. The guard was wounded in the attack. Islamic radicals have since called for Geller's head, and vow to kill anyone who blessed themes Muhammad. Muhammad is a butcher that had sex with a pig, how's that. Please look at my Muhammad cartoons in the back.

May 10 Macedonia, Kumanovo 8 murdered and 37 injured. Muslim terrorists wage a running battle with police, murdered at least eight.

Jun. 21 Austria, Graz 3 murdered and 34 injured. A 4-year-old boy is among three slain in a shopping district by a 'mentally ill' Muslim with a stated interest in Jihad.

Jun. 26 France, Lyon 1 murdered and 2 injured. A 'normal Muslim' attacks a factory, beheads one worker and raises the Islamist flag after hoisting the severed head on a fence.

July 16 2015, Four U.S. Marines have been shot dead in an attack, reported by a lone Islamic gunman, on U.S. Navy facilities in Chattanooga, Tennessee. Chattanooga mayor, Andy Berke said five people died in all, including the gunman. Two law enforcement sources told CBS News that the shooting suspect was identified as Muhammad Youssef Abdulazeez, 24. Abdulazeez was born in Kuwait an immigrated to the U.S. where he reportedly became a naturalized U.S. citizen. The FBI is investigating two crime scenes, a navy recruiting center at a strip mall where the first shots were fired, and a navy reserve center about 7 miles away. More than 100 rounds were reportedly fired in a shootout with police at the recruitment center parking lot. The shooter then drove to the navy reserve center and started shooting Marines, four of whom were murdered. The marines would not have been armed at a reserve Navy installation or at a recruitment center, both of which were described as soft targets. The four Marines who were fatally shot were reportedly were attached at the navy reserve center on Amnicola highway. A police officer at the first location was injured and was being treated at a local hospital for a gunshot wound to the ankle. We are conducting this as an act of domestic terrorism said Bill Killian, U.S. Attorney for Tennessee at A 3:00 PM press conference. He came back to the podium 15 minutes later and backtracked, telling reporters I would encourage you not to get caught up in labels, whether it was an act of terrorism or crime.

Aug. 20 Russia, Pyatigorsk 1 murdered. A moderate imam is assassinated by more radical co-religionists.

Aug. 21 France, Paris 3 injured. A Muslim trained by ISIS opens fire with a Kalashnikov on a train before being subdued by unarmed American passengers.

Sept. 14 England, White Chapel 1 murdered. A faith healer is stabbed to death in a targeted attack by a religious Muslim.

Sept. 17 Germany, Berlin 1 injured. An Islamic extremist stabs a policewoman in the neck.

Sept. 29 Denmark, Copenhagen 1 injured. A Palestinian ISIS sympathizer stabs a policeman at a refugee center.

Oct. 7 Germany, Dessau 1 murdered. A young refugee is honor murdered on the order of her family after being gang-raped in Syria.

Oct. 24 France, Marseille 2 injured. A man yelling 'Allah Akbar' attacks a rabbi in a synagogue and stabs another Jew trying to help.

Nov. 12 Italy, Milan 1 injured. A Haredi Jew is stabbed nine times by a masked Muslim.

Nov. 13 France, Paris 89 murdered and 322 injured. Islamic terrorists open fire and throw bombs during a concert at a music hall, slaughtering nearly ninety innocents while shouting 'Allah Akbar' (Bataclan).

Nov. 13 France, Paris 5 murdered and 8 injured. Islamic terrorists shoot up a bar and pizzeria, murdered five patrons (La Bonne Biere, Casa Nostra).

Nov. 13 France, Paris 15 murdered and 10 injured. Islamic terrorists massacre fifteen innocents at two restaurants (Le Carillon and Le Petit Cambodge).

Nov. 13 France, Paris 1 murdered. Islamic terrorists eliminate a passerby with two suicide blasts outside a soccer stadium (Stade de France).

Nov. 13 France, Paris 3 injured. Islamic terrorists stage a suicide bombing outside a cafe Comptoir Voltaire).

Nov. 13 France, Paris 19 murdered and 9 injured. Islamic terrorists pile up nineteen bodies at a restaurant (Belle Equipe). Islamic shit like this is what will destroy the restaurant businesses make no mistake Congress.

Nov. 18 France, Marseille 1 injured. A Jewish teacher is stabbed by 'radicalized' Muslims.

Dec. 5 England, London 3 injured. A Muslim with a machete slashes commuters at a subway station.

Dec. 28 Georgia, Tbilisi 1 murdered. A 22-year-old Shiite is stabbed to death by a Salafi over 'religious hatred'.

2016

Jan. 1 France, Valence 2 injured. Two other people are injured when a Muslim deliberately rams French guards outside a mosque.

Jan. 11 France, Marseille 1 injured. A Jewish teacher is attacked with a machete 'in the name of Allah.'

Jan. 27 Sweden, Tanum 1 murdered. A 60-year-old man is stabbed to death by one of his employees after being accused of 'Islamophobia'...

Feb. 18 England, Rochdale 1 murdered. A popular imam is beaten to death by ISIS supporters.

Feb. 26 Germany, Hanover 1 injured. A 'radicalized' teen girl stabs a female police officer.

Feb. 29 Russia, Moscow 1 murdered. A woman beheads a child, saying that it was revenge for 'spilled Muslim blood' in Syria.

Mar. 22 Belgium, Brussels 21 murdered and 130 injured. A Religion of Peace suicide blast on a subway train incinerates twenty-one commuters.

Mar. 22 Belgium, Brussels 14 murdered and 92 injured. Fourteen people are murdered when two suicide bombers detonate nail-packed explosives at crowded airline counters.

Mar. 24 Scotland, Glasgow 1 murdered. An Ahmadi minority is stabbed to death by a radical Muslim over his religious beliefs.

Apr. 16 Germany, Essen 3 injured. ISIS-inspired teens bomb a Sikh wedding.

May 10 Germany, Grafing 1 murdered and 3 injured. A man shouting praises to Allah stabs four commuters at a train station.

May 19 Germany, Baden-Württemberg, 1 murdered. A 70-year-old woman is murdered in her home by a young Muslim who leaves a 'religious' note at the scene.

May 20 England, London 4 injured. A Turkish man yelling about Lee Rigby stabs four women in a parking lot on the third anniversary.

May 27 France, Saint Julien du Puy 1 injured. An off-duty soldier is stabbed by ISIS supporters while jogging.

Jun. 13 France, Magnanville 2 murdered and 1 injured. A terrorist stabs a couple to death while shouting praises to Allah.

Jun. 14 Belgium, Etterbeek 1 injured. A transgender is stabbed by religious radicals.

July 14 France, Nice 86 murdered and 202 injured. A Muslim migrant mows down eighty-six Bastille Day revelers (including ten children) with a truck while shouting praises to Allah.

July 18 Germany, Wuerzburg 5 injured. A 'refugee' with an axe hacks at people on a train while screaming 'Allah Akbar'

July 19 France, Garda-Colombe 4 injured. A mother and her three young daughters are stabbed by a Muslim man during breakfast for not being sufficiently clothed.

July 24 Germany, Ansbach 15 injured. A Syrian 'asylum seeker' detonates a nail-packed suicide bomb at a wine bar outside a music festival.

July 26 France, Saint-Etienne-du-Rouvray 1 murdered and 1 injured. Muslim radicals take hostages at a church and slit the throat of an 84-year-old priest.

Aug. 4 England, London 1 murdered and 5 injured. A Somali migrant goes on a stabbing spree, murdered an American woman.

Aug. 6 Belgium, Charleroi 2 injured. A man attacks two female police officers with a machete while praising Allah.

Aug. 19 France, Strasbourg 1 injured. A rabbi in orthodox clothing is stabbed by a man shouting praises to Allah.

Aug. 27 Germany, Oberhausen 2 injured. A couple enjoying a picnic are brutally stabbed by a man shouting praises to Allah.

Aug. 30 France, Toulouse 1 injured. A young female police officer is stabbed by a Muslim in a planned attack.

Aug. 31 Denmark, Christiania 3 injured. Two cops and a civilian are shot by a Bosnian-born Muslim with ties to ISIS.

Sept. 2 France, Vincennes 1 injured. A Muslim radical stabs a police officer.

Sept. 3 France, Belfort 2 injured. Islamists savagely beat a writer and his son over a book about Jihad.

Sept. 4 France, Osny, 2 injured. A Muslim radical stabs two prison guards.

Sept. 7 Belgium, Brussels 2 injured. A Muslim man attacks two police officers with a knife.

Sept. 8 France, Boussy-Saint-Antoine 1 injured. A Muslim woman stabs a police officer after planting explosives outside a cathedral.

Sept. 26 Russia, Kara-Tyube 1 murdered. A moderate Imam is shot dead by radical co-religionists.

Oct. 5 Belgium, Brussels 2 injured. A man stabs two police officer while shouting in Arabic.

Oct. 16 Germany, Hamburg 1 murdered and 1 injured. Two German teens are stabbed by a 'radicalized' Muslim while sitting below a bridge

Dec. 19 Germany, Berlin 12 murdered and 48 injured. A dozen patrons are slaughtered when a hijacked truck plows into a crowd at a Christmas market outside a church.

The list of horrific atrocities is endless everyday a Mosque exists anywhere in the world. The revisions of this book will surpass any historical book previously published in thickness and number of pages in the near future if Congress does nothing to stop the spread of Islam. Lawrence Lueder, January 2016

FOREIGN TERRORIST ORGANIZATIONS

Read what the fuck they do to murder innocent people around the world and all of these ass-hole Islamic organizations worship the Butcher Muhammad and believe the Quran is the word of Allah. Ghee, how many such terrorist groups exist in the United States that Congress fails to see that Islam has a problem??? Read about each one at the following link: https://www.state.gov/documents/organization/65479.pdf .

Abu Nidal Organization (ANO) Abu Sayyaf Group (ASG) Al-Aqsa Martyrs Brigade Ansar al-Sunna (AS) Armed Islamic Group (GIA) Asbat al-Ansar Aum Shinrikyo (Aum) Basque Fatherland and Liberty (ETA) Communist Party of Philippines/New People's Army (CPP/NPA) Continuity Irish Republican Army (CIRA) Gama'a al-Islamiyya (IG) HAMAS Harakat ul-Mujahedin (HUM) Hizballah Islamic Jihad Group (IJU) Islamic Movement of Uzbekistan (IMU) Jaish-e-Mohammed (JEM) Jemaah Islamiya Organization (JI) Al-Jihad (AJ) Kahane Chai (Kach) Kongra-Gel (KGK) Lashkar e-Tayyiba (LT) Lashkar i Jhangvi (LJ) Liberation Tigers of Tamil Eelam (LTTE) Libyan Islamic Fighting Group (LIFG) Moroccan Islamic Combatant Group (GICM) Mujahedin-e Khalq Organization (MEK) National Liberation Army (ELN) Palestine Liberation Front (PLF) Palestinian Islamic Jihad (PIJ) Popular Front for the Liberation of Palestine (PFLP) Popular Front for the Liberation of Palestine-General Command (PFLP-GC) Al-Qaida (AQ) Al-Qaida in Iraq (AQI) Real IRA (RIRA) Revolutionary Armed Forces of Colombia (FARC) Revolutionary Nuclei (RN) Revolutionary Organization 17 November Revolutionary People's Liberation Party/Front (DHKP/C) Salafist Group for Preaching and Combat (GSPC) Shining Path (SL) United Self-Defense Forces of Colombia (AUC)

I counted **42** terrorist organizations, most of them Muslim. Now if the whites in the America had this many, Washington would do everything in its power to shut them down as they did the KKK and other such organizations.

Let us not forget that when the Negros used the Black Panthers to enforce law and order in their neighborhoods, for some reason they were accepted by the Black communities and it worked, violence and murder went down wherever they patrolled. Now, if the KKK was doing the same for white neighborhoods, who's to say that wasn't working. Muslims follow a similar code of ethics, the Sharia laws and somehow Washington blindly assumes that over time Muslims will be more accepted. Muslims do not have the same dilemma that Blacks do for being accepted, many Muslims are light skin colored and are assumed to be like others in our society. The only thing keeping them from becoming part of society is Muslims believing in a repressive order, which intertwines Constitutional order. Freedom means just that and the United States should not accommodate anyone that restricts freedom. Women in states like Utah repress women, however not to the degree Muslims do and all of it needs to cease. No one should repress anyone, adults are not children that require a restrictive set of rules to live by and the people in Washington should address such issues.

Hopefully, the Saudi that started it all with Madrassas, repressive schools that teach hatred and the memorizing of the evil book of the Quran, are now pondering ways to ease off force teaching without appearing guilty of sponsoring the birth of Islamic terrorism. Let us hope...

I just watched some news (March 2017) from England, and it was about hundreds of Muslims leaving Islam for Christianity or atheism. All of the persons they interviewed were afraid for their life. Anytime, someone in America threatens another person with death threats that person often are arrested. Why is the Quran, a written threat taught to every Muslim child allowed to exist, only to have our presidents say when it happens, we didn't see it coming? **What is America doing to protect people that wish to leave any religion? This is proof that the First Amendment regarding religion is due for some clarifications.**

White Americans, KKK, Skin Heads etc.

The only way for Americans to protect themselves from Muslims that can spontaneously decide to murder them, meaning you the reader, is for Americans (non-Muslims) to arm themselves to the teeth. Make no mistake; Islam is like a slow moving mudslide that will, eventually cover you up until you are dead if not stopped. Moreover, like most landslides, Public Works (Our Government) does not react until disaster has struck. Do not wait to be murdered by some nut job Muslims that gets angry over something we feel is freedom. Washington has demonstrated many times over, to react after an attack and hardly ever before an attack, recall Pearl Harbor or 9/11 nothing has changed. Do not wait for political correctness to have caused the murder of another innocent life in America. In addition, anyone that does business with Muslims should also understand that they might also be contributing to the death of an innocent person or many people. Just as Christians support their church of love and peace, Muslims support mosques where Mullahs teach death to Americans, repression of women and pedophilia is acceptable. I believe the worst we've seen from Catholics is pedophilia and no mass killings.

A wake up call for Congress to react to Muslim aggression, I suggest the KKK, the Skin Heads, The Hells Angels, or any White person that is in a gang should consider registering as a religion. As a religion, your organization will be free from taxes, and you would be allowed to carry weapons, do whatever drugs you please, as do some Native American Indians or whatever they are called these days. You can even restrict minorities from your areas of influence, as do the Muslims when they prevent conversion to other religions in their Mosques, or use intimidation to take over areas like whole neighborhood streets. You can even form a religion that exists to simply burn the Quran and exists to draw cartoons of the Butcher Muhammad. Heck, I believe Scientology is nothing more than an organization for the rich to hide their wealth; no one seems to know what those nut jobs are doing in the desert, where a gigantic so-called church compound is being built.

Get over it; we are all racist to some degree with borders, gated communities, religions or special schools. Society can tolerate small percentages of individuals of different color, religion or affiliations. However, once that percentage goes up in a race in specific areas, society will fight back.

Lawrence Lueder 2017.

I'll be publishing another book regarding what's wrong with mixing races. Look for it; it is a revelation you do not want to miss. It is time to cease being politically correct for once. Doubt it, then checkout YouTube on such subjects.

Why would anyone worship a prophet that cut off the heads of some 600 innocent men? It took Muhammad three days to cut off all those heads. How can Washington allow such a religious cult to exist in the free America? And we thought the Aztec were crazy evil people.

The Title of my Book

My book title is to awaken the world to the truth. Anyone that provides a weapon to a known murderer often goes to jail in America and in many other parts of the world. The American presidents since Eisenhower all supplied not one gun, but billions of dollars in weapons to known governments that were repressing their people, committing murder often in secrecy, and many other illegal activities. The American Presidents need to be held accountable by the World Court or by the American court system for treason. If not then perhaps they should be sued in Civil Court. It was all done so that arms dealers could get rich while funding the presidential elections thereby ensuring their presidential win. None of the Muslim countries required protection to that degree as America was supplying, because protection was being provided by the American taxpayers with Navy Ships patrolling the Middle East Seas and much more. The arms deals to Muslim Countries are what caused the murdering of thousands of our military soldiers. The United States was supposed to be setting an example. Instead, it was every president, from Eisenhower up to Obama, for himself. Each President once in office got rich as quickly as possible while in office, even at the cost of our troops dying fighting against Muslims that were armed by the same Presidents, Commander in Chief. Moreover, how did they do that? By sleeping with the enemy, in this case it was the silent enemy hiding behind the first amendment of the constitution. This is about presidents getting rich on the blood of our soldiers, who died for no reason other than to protect arms dealers and oil rich evil sheik.

Because Islam was allowed to enter the US, Americans have to be alert 24/7. No one should feel uncomfortable wherever they visit in the US. However, recent attacks throughout Europe are proving that Muslims are making life extremely dangerous for places to visit and shop. No other religion is causing such ills for every country in the world except Islam and it needs to be squash immediately.

To remain silent is what has allowed repressive religions and regimes to exist. As long as a single Muslim exists in America, Americans are not free. *Lawrence A. Lueder 2017.*

Cartoons

MUHAMMAD THE BUTCHER

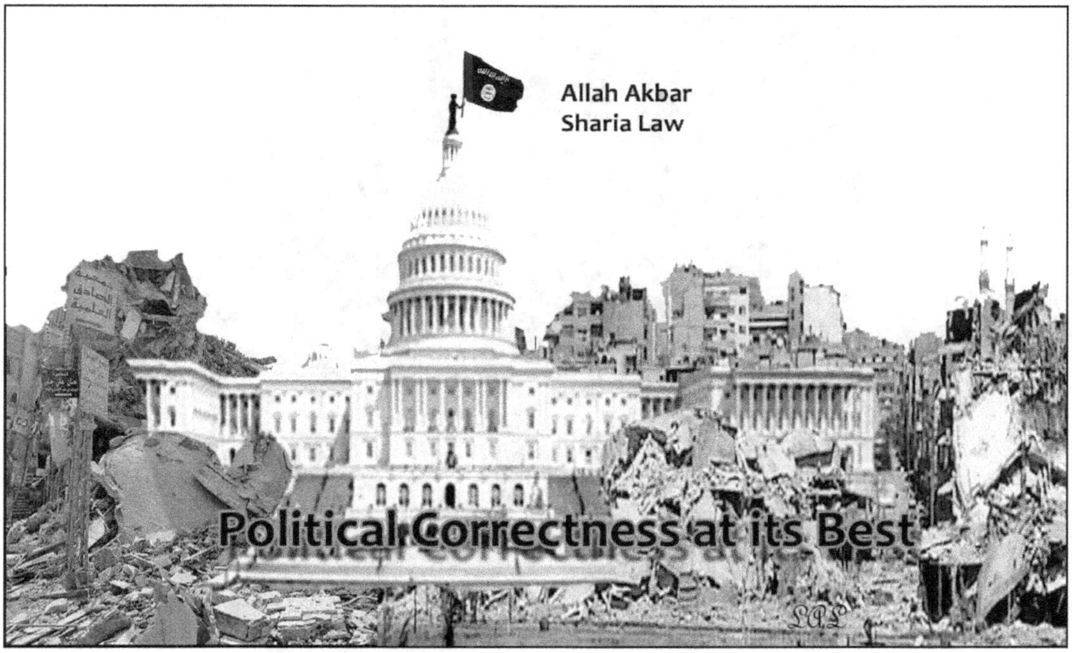

WASHINGTON CAPITAL WHEN MUSLIMS TAKE OVER.

The Saudi know this guy

Ben Laden, I see why they called you, Dick Face.

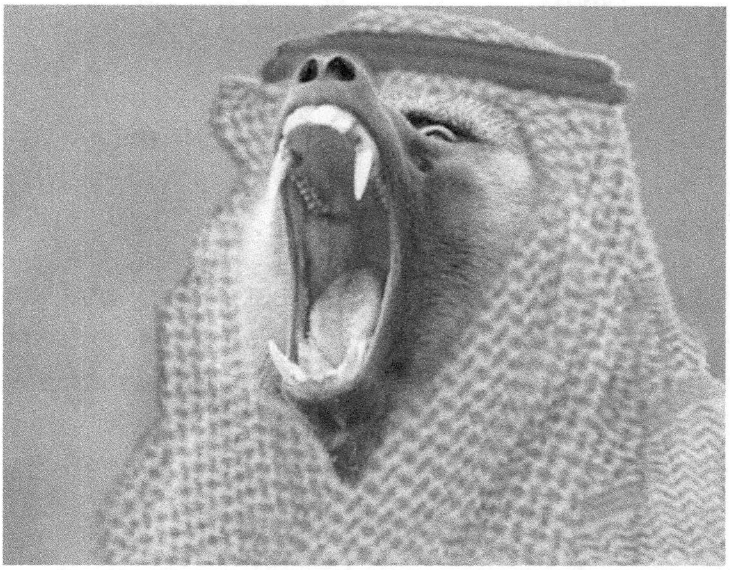

Since no one knows what Muhammad looks like, May I suggest...

They forgot to mention to the suicide bombers that the virgins all looked alike with pig like noses.

Contributors' lists thank you all. There may be some others I missed, keep up the fight against Islam. The Truth

www.wnd.com,

www.thereligionofpeace.com

www.ilovemyfredon.org

Please visit the website, The Religion of Peace, they have roughly 98 pages of Muslim attacks just for the year 2015, there was too many pages for me to enter them all and make this book affordable.

This book is my third warning to the military to be on alert of any Muslims in the armed forces; failure is the result of Fort Hood. I had warned the Navy that it was going to happened, and no one took my advice. I also advise anyone that is harmed by a Muslim should use this book as a reference, and go after the politically correct politicians in a civil suit. Peace does not come without a fight. No more politicians should get rich from the deaths of our boys that fought Muslims.

A hero is anyone that burns the Quran, or better yet, burns or tears one up in front of a Mosque.

A coward is he that remains silent against the evils of Islam just like the Jews did when Hitler came to power. There is no difference between Sharia and any other Muslim religious cult; they are all, evil, repressive in their entirety.

Just imagine how much America could advance if it did not have to be on alert from Muslim attacks every day and everywhere. It has become a hundred Billion dollar loss to Americans every year that another mosque exists in the Free World.

If you still do not believe, our ex-presidents were big-time ass-holes, just remember that all of them armed Muslims, and not once was the Vatican given any protection, or arms. No other religion is so armed to the teeth as Islamic terrorists by ex-presidents.

Our soldiers die in the Middle East not because of terrorist Muslims; it's because of our presidents arming the killers of your sons to get RICH.

I feel you can help by not attending any college with Islamic professors, stay away from Muslim shops and hotels until Congress can prove Islam is a religion and not some evil cult. Supporting Muslims, you support death to innocent people; it all goes to justifying Islam.

www.ingramcontent.com/pod-product-compliance
Lightning Source LLC
Chambersburg PA
CBHW081406280526
45788CB00009B/2998
* 9 7 8 1 5 4 4 0 0 8 6 1 5 *